"As a pastor, I find that Christians almost always don't know how to handle their grief. Do we hide it stoically, pretending we're OK or do we allow our emotions to run their course? This is why I wholeheartedly recommend *Aftermath: Growing in Grace Through Grief.* My dear friend Margaret McSweeney shares an honest story of her own journey through the losses of loved ones. I know nobody who has endured the trials of life with more grace. Purchase this book and keep it for those unexpected moments and purchase another copy for the friend who sorrows."

—Daniel Darling, senior pastor and author of
iFaith: Connecting with God in the 21st Century

"I'm so grateful Margaret has written this much-needed book. Her transparency is inviting and her true compassion is disarming. I found that when her stories were layered on top of mine, a depth of clarity came into view. I felt a hope and a comfort that had been incomplete during my recent journey with sorrow. For anyone who has experienced loss, this book will be a tender companion. You will find yourself encircled with a hug from heaven, as Margaret calls it. Best of all, you will be surprised when you discover the hidden gem of God's grace in the midst of the grief."

—Robin Jones Gunn, best-selling author of *Cottage by the Sea*

"In her book *Aftermath: Growing in Grace Through Grief,* Margaret McSweeney offers a touching and intimate portrait of a personal journey through grief, offering the reader spiritual insights, compassionate counsel and, most important of all, hope and healing. This heartfelt book offers a pathway to grace."
—SUSAN DOLAN, RN, BSN, JD, EXECUTIVE DIRECTOR, ANGELS GRACE HOSPICE, BOLINGBROOK, ILLINOIS, AND COAUTHOR OF *END OF LIFE ADVISOR: PERSONAL, LEGAL, AND MEDICAL CONSIDERATIONS FOR A PEACEFUL, DIGNIFIED DEATH*

Growing in Grace Through Grief

aftermath

MARGARET McSWEENEY

With excerpts from When Grief Is Your Constant Companion,
by Carolyn Rhea, Margaret's mother

NEW HOPE
PUBLISHERS
Gospel-Centered. Missions-Driven.

BIRMINGHAM, ALABAMA

New Hope® Publishers
P. O. Box 12065
Birmingham, AL 35202-2065
NewHopeDigital.com

New Hope Publishers is a division of WMU®.

Library of Congress Cataloging-in-Publication Data
McSweeney, Margaret.

  Aftermath : growing in grace through grief / Margaret McSweeney.
    p. cm.
  ISBN 978-1-59669-343-2 (pbk.)
  1. Grief--Religious aspects--Christianity. I. Title.
  BV4905.3.M37 2012
  248.8'66--dc23
                               2012014167

ISBN-10: 1-59669-343-6
ISBN-13: 978-1-59669-343-2

N124148· 0712 · 2.5M1

Table of Contents

Dedication

"PRAY"LUDE
Shadows of the Almighty
Almighty God, thy greatness
Is beyond the grasp of my frail mind;
Yet deep within there is this yearning
To seek and find thee for myself.
I stumble in Earth's darkness.
My soul cries out for light.
These human eyes are not conditioned
For the blinding light
Of thy glorious presence,
But perhaps they could discern
Thy shadow touching Earth.
Break through with light, O God!
I cannot see even a shadow
Unless there is some light![1]
— CAROLYN RHEA

Dedicated in loving memory to my father, Dr. Claude H. Rhea Jr., my mother, Carolyn Rhea, and my brother, Randy.

Acknowledgments

The two words "thank you" cannot adequately express my heartfelt gratitude to those who have accompanied me, comforted me, prayed for me and provided counsel as I completed this emotional project.

Thank you, *Dave*. You are my beloved husband, and your constant love, support, and encouragement throughout my journey of grief and during the process of writing this book are indeed eternal blessings.

Thank you, *Melissa* and *Katie*. God has truly blessed me with precious daughters. Your loving kindness and patience have allowed me to spend the necessary time to write this book.

Thank you, *Claude*. You are a wonderful big brother, and I value your godly guidance. Mother and Daddy would be so proud of you.

Thank you, *Elaine*. I will be forever grateful that you shared my brother Randy's miraculous testimony with me.

Thank you, *Andrea Mullins*. I would never have written this book without your gentle insistence and constant prayers.

Thank you, *Joyce Dinkins*. Your graciousness has been such a gift.

Thank you, *Janet Grant*, my literary agent and founder of Books & Such Literary Agency. I appreciate your encouragement as I continue to grow as a writer.

Thank you to those who shared their wise counsel on grief in this book: *Rich Blue, Dr. Gary Chapman, Dr. F. William Chapman, Dr. Harrell Cushing, Pastor Daniel Darling, Jennifer Degler, Ray Ercoli, Pastor Rob Jackson, The Rev. Russell J. Levenson Jr, Pastor Mike MacIntosh, Timothy Owings, Bro. Kevin Tuggle, Sr., Austin Ward, Nancy Williams,* and *Pastor Don Wink.*

Additional heartfelt thanks to dear friends and family members who helped me along my difficult journey: *May, Melanie, Kathy, Kim, Denise, Lori, Patricia, Lisa, Julie, Robin, Tricia, Amy, Rita, Vicky, Bonnie, Felicia, Anna, Sandra, Jeanette, Peggy, Kathy D., Pastor Jane, Stacie, Elizabeth, Mary, Kelley, Julie M. Linda, Jan, Mary K., Sarah, Lisa J., Dawn, Mrs. Wilson, Mrs. Bray, Mrs. White,* fellow Pearl Girls, my church family from Atonement, and church school friends from Immanuel Lutheran, my church family from Mountain Brook Baptist, friends from Samford University and University of South Carolina, and many, many others. You are indeed such blessings in my life.

And thank you, dear reader, for taking the time to pick up this book. My thoughts and prayers are with you during your difficult journey of grief. May your footsteps of faith lead you to a closer walk and relationship with the heavenly Father.

"Praise be to the *God and Father of our Lord Jesus Christ*, the Father of compassion and the God of all comfort, who comforts us in all our troubles, so that we can comfort those in any trouble with the comfort we ourselves have received from God." (1 Corinthians 1:3–4)

Introduction

"Lord, are You sure that I am supposed to write this book?"

Expecting to sip from a refreshing water fountain, I instead encountered the powerful blast of a fire hydrant. Grief does that. Many times, I had to physically step away from my computer and distance myself from the painful encounters of saying "good-bye" yet again to my parents and to my brother Randy.

New Hope publisher Andrea Mullins asked me to share my personal journey of grief. New Hope had published my mother's ninth and final book, *When Grief Is My Constant Companion: God's Grace for a Woman's Heartache,* in 2003 — mere months before my mother passed away from an aggressive form of leukemia. Andrea encouraged me to write this book as if singing a duet with my parents a la Nat King Cole and Natalie Cole performing "Unforgettable." I reminded her that my dad's God-given musical talent skipped me and that I could barely carry a tune. However, I was intrigued by the concept of intertwining my individual grief experience within the lessons of faith my parents' lives had taught me through the years. How hard could this be? I would just share my thoughts along with my mother's writings. No problem. I was not prepared, however, for the actual plans God had for me and for this book.

My workbook of grief ultimately became a means of healing by revealing, and as a very private person I wrestled with the direction in which I felt the Lord was leading me with this book. It was way too personal. "Lord, are you sure I'm supposed to write this book?" my heart cried out to Him countless times. "Can I really share with the world that for most of my life my mother and I were not very close? Do I really have to reveal that I didn't really know my mother beyond her role of 'Mother' until I started writing this book?"

This book overflows with my mother's words of faith, fear and frustration throughout her life. Many of her words were previously published; many words were written privately to family and friends; and some words have never been read until I opened her private journals. Through her stacks of letters to my dad, I got to know my mother as a young woman who was in love, and I read about her dreams for life with my dad. Through her private journal entries, I got to know my mother as a sometimes frustrated middle-aged wife who struggled to rediscover and reclaim her own identity. Through writings in her Spiritual Health Record notebook, I got to know my mother as a persistent prayer warrior who also carried the burden of self-inflicted guilt and perceived failure as a mother. Through underlined verses and scribbled notes in the margins of her Bible and devotional books, I got to know my mother as a child of God whose deeply rooted faith in Him held strong even during the deluge of life's storms. Through passages from my mother's many published books, I got to know my mother as an author. And through the pages of her final book, I got to know my mother as a fellow traveler along the path of grief, trying to reconcile faith with the human intensity of grief and reach an ultimate place of peace — in our heavenly Father's arms. As a result of getting to know my mother and struggling to write this book, I became even closer to the One who is the Author and Finisher of our faith.

As you will soon discover, personal letters are widely featured throughout the chapters. I feel humbled and blessed to have these typed and handwritten notes from my parents and grandparents. They have become generational footprints of faith to guide me along the path of grief. And in sharing these letters, I pray that they will minister God's grace to you as well. It's so interesting that God uses letters to spread His word and comfort to those who suffer.

The New Testament contains 21 epistles, or letters, written to individuals, groups and churches.

Writing this book has felt almost like writing a letter to you, dear reader. We may not know each other, but we understand the emotions that we share through the journey of grief. Perhaps you are the one grieving right now or you know someone who is going through a difficult time, and you are trying to find a way to reach out and help. No matter what the circumstance is, my heartfelt prayer is that you will find comfort and experience God's grace as I share my family's writings and God's Words with you.

Let's say a prayer together before this journey.

Dear Heavenly Father,

Thank You for the incredible opportunity to come to You in prayer. We praise You, Father and recognize all that You have done for us. Thank You for knowing our names and the plans that You have for us. You know the specific sorrow that each of us holds in our hearts. You know that as humans the journey through grief can sometimes feel unbearable to us. You know our needs before we even are able to articulate them. Please draw near to us as we journey through these very difficult times. Please let us feel your loving Presence and hold us close to You.

And Lord, please be especially close to those readers who are desperately seeking comfort and answers. Please provide the necessary strength and assurance that they need to make this difficult journey through grief. May the words that are penned upon the pages be a blessing to them, and may Your Holy Spirit lead them to the sections of the book that will best minister to them. May they fully experience the grace, peace and love found through Your Son, Jesus Christ in whose name we ask these things. Amen.

Chapter 1

Grief Needs No Introduction

Volcanic Soil
Sudden loss
Like molten lava
Has wiped out what I love.
Now I am desolate.
Grief has no words to pray
And yet I seek our God in prayer,
For there is hope only in Him.
In His presence
I plant my tiny mustard seed of faith
in grief's volcanic soil
And leave it in His loving care.[1]
— CAROLYN RHEA

"Your father is dead."

On September 19, 1990, my mother's words crashed through my life. I pushed aside the files stacked on my desk in my small cubicle and pressed the phone against my ear. The fast-paced life of corporate finance transactions in a New York City bank became a distant distraction. "He had a massive heart attack at the Charles de Gaulle Airport in Paris."

I bit my trembling lip. "Mother, I need to call you back from the conference room." Maybe it was reflexes from my Southern upbringing, but I didn't want others to observe my emotional breakdown. I needed to be alone. I raced across the hallway into the conference room with its massive, polished wood table and rolling chairs neatly lined beneath the veneer. I stood at the credenza and quickly dialed my mother's number. My parents had been living in West Palm Beach, Florida for over eight years. She answered the phone and was in tears. I didn't ask her to repeat what she had told me before. I knew my dad was dead. I tried to stay strong and comfort her. "Dave and I will fly to Florida tonight. We're on our way. We'll work through this. I love you."

Fortunately, my fiancé, Dave, also worked at the bank. I called him through the interoffice line. "Daddy's dead." I sobbed. Dave rushed to my floor and held me close as my tears soaked into his Brooks Brothers suit. As we walked together to the elevator, my contacts flew out of my eyes due to my crying. At that moment my life became a blur in many ways.

On the airplane, Dave held onto my hand. Memories, like a flock of migrating birds, swarmed across my mind. As the youngest child and only daughter in the family, I had always felt like the apple of my daddy's eye. We were close, and I adored him. His life lessons instilled in me a heart for charity and a belief that an individual can make a difference in the world while honoring God. After my piano lesson at age ten, we had walked down the hallway of the Music School at Samford University where he was then dean. The custodian was mopping the floor. My dad stopped to talk with him and for several minutes asked about this man's family members by name. Driving home, my dad turned down the classical music station and said, "Always remember to treat everyone with the same respect whether he or she is a janitor or the President of the United States."

My dad accomplished so much during his short life span of 62 years. As a lyric tenor, he had recorded five albums with Word; one was even with the London Concert Orchestra. He was a college president, a fellow of the Royal Society of the Arts, a former dean, a colon cancer survivor, but most importantly, he was an amazing father. As an awkward teen, I did not date much in high school, but my dad always made me feel beautiful and would sometimes take me out on a special daddy/daughter dinner date at an elegant place that featured a live orchestra and ballroom dancing. He was a modern-day Renaissance man who simultaneously embraced the fine arts and strategic leadership responsibilities. When I was in high school, my dad even went to work late one morning so he could prepare homemade crepes to serve to my French class. My dad modeled a loving marriage, even though it could be embarrassing at times. On a dateless Friday evening, I was in the backseat of the car with one of my friends when my dad burst into a German love song and serenaded my blushing mother in the front seat. He was unashamedly in love with my mother and cooked gourmet meals for her all the time.

During Labor Day weekend, only a week before my dad's death, I flew from New York to West Palm Beach to plan my wedding. He loved Dave like a son, which was really special since Dave had lost his dad when he was a teenager. And he enjoyed telling his friends how Dave had called him one afternoon from the board room of a large corporation in Los Angeles to ask for my hand in marriage.

I hugged my dad good-bye at West Palm Beach International Airport. Since he was heading to Paris a few days later on a business trip, my final words to him were *"good-bye!"* How fitting that I said, "Have a good trip," not realizing that his final destination would be heaven.

The aftermath of losing my father was instant. Immediate decisions had to be made: How do we transport his body back from Paris? What would be the funeral arrangements? Do I still move forward with my wedding? Where will my mother live?

Grief can change life in an instant, and for many of us, grief leaves a calling card: a huge hole. A cavity. An abyss. Sometimes the remnant of our shattered lives teeters on the edge of a personal Grand Canyon. How do we regain balance? How do we regain hope? How do we rebuild? And where is God? Even as devout Christians, we can still encounter these emotional questions, and that's OK.

Grief left an even deeper personal abyss a few years ago. On April 15, 2003, I became an adult orphan. What an odd pairing of words. Adult orphan. Why would that be so difficult? Parents are supposed to die. That's the cycle of life. Yes. That is the typical cycle; however, when my parents died, it felt more like a cyclone than a natural unfolding of events.

My mother lived for 13 years after my dad died until she lost a brief battle with leukemia in 2003. Although her death was expected, the aftermath was unexpected. My emotional rollercoaster ranged from separation anxiety to guilt, anger, sorrow and at last acceptance.

My mother and I had a longer time to say good-bye. I would fly to Florida from Chicago to care for her every other week or so while my husband and his niece Kelley cared for our young daughters.

During those last few months, I became really close to my mother. To be quite candid, I was never as close to my mother as I was to my dad. I loved her, but we were different in many ways. My father was always ready with a hug and ebullient words of praise for me. He constantly encouraged me to pursue my dreams and challenge myself. My mother, however, was a bit more formal and reserved in expressing her love during my childhood and adolescence. Unlike my dad, my mother never quite understood my decision to major in international business, learn Portuguese, live in Brazil and work in New York City. However, she supported me with her constant prayers and even visited me in Rio de Janeiro. My mother and I didn't fully connect until my 30s when

I started writing. She became my mentor. We talked on the phone constantly, and I would read my latest poem or chapter out loud to her. We had found a common connecting point: Words from our heart to honor the Lord. I encouraged her to submit to a publisher her writings about becoming a widow. In 2003, at the same time she was diagnosed with an aggressive form of leukemia, New Hope published my mother's book, *When Grief Is Your Constant Companion: God's Grace for a Woman's Heartache,* a book that shares my mother's tumultuous journey through grief after losing my dad. She writes about her emotions with such heart-wrenching candor and raw emotion while drawing upon her deep faith to sustain her. Within the pages of this book, I too will share candid experiences of becoming an adult orphan juxtaposed to the landmarks of my mother's journey through loss.

A major challenge in writing this book was figuring out the best way to organize everything. Grief is messy. I can't neatly wrap the process of grief inside a package. How can one put decorative tissue paper around a wrecking ball? I needed to find a format that would provide a working foundation for understanding the grief process. In her book *Death and Dying,* Elisabeth Kubler-Ross categorizes the following stages of grief:

- **D**enial (this isn't *happening* to me!)
- **A**nger (why is this happening to *me?*)
- **B**argaining (I promise I'll be a better person *if* . . .)
- **D**epression (I don't *care* anymore)
- **A**cceptance (I'm *ready* for whatever comes)

Honestly, I don't think grief can be pigeonholed into stages. Not everyone goes through the same stages in sequential order. Ray Ercoli, former director of programs and workshops at Willow Creek Community Church, suggests that "emotions of grief" is a more accurate depiction. A stage implies a beginning and an end, but emotions can be circular. Something can trigger feelings of anger or depression, and you can feel those feelings again and again.

For simplicity's sake, however, this book will be divided into the five common emotions of grief. I will include excerpts from my mother's book *When Grief Is Your Constant Companion*, along with treasured family letters, journal entries and my own thoughts. Generational footprints of faith have paved a pathway to lead to a place of grace where God calls each of us from our ledges of darkness and invites us to renew our life and purpose.

This book is intended to be an interactive process in which you, too, will share your heart and discover some tangible handles to get through your grief and glimpse God's grace through your journey. I've consulted some experts to glean their wisdom and advice about dealing with these tumultuous emotions of loss. And of course God's own words will provide the ultimate sense of comfort.

My heartfelt prayer is that you will feel God's gentle arms around you as He leads you away from the darkness and into the Light of His Word. And may your tear-filled eyes see the difficult path in front of you through the lens of faith. Inspired by the front cover of my mother's final book, I penned the poem on the following page after she died. It was my first "faith step" of my personal journey through grief.

Vision of Faith

As waves splash and play games of tag,
I navigate around each crag,
Stepping alone since you walked ahead
To wear a robe of eternal thread.
I strain my eyes and try to see
Glimpses of you in eternity.
My vision though has earthly sight
With boundaries of horizon's light.
Through a lens of faith, there's clarity;
With outstretched arms, you wait for me
Your presence will always be a guide
As I finish my walk on this side.[2]
— Margaret McSweeney

"The Lord replied, 'My Presence will go with you, and I will give you rest.'" Exodus 33:14 (NIV)

Shock ··· Shock ··· Shock

Chapter 2

Like lightning, grief strikes my life.
Its piercing impact momentarily paralyzes my mind,
*   but soon the reality of loss shatters the numbness*
*   with torrents of despair.*
At last the downpour diminishes to a drizzle. The
*   thundercloud passes; the sky clears — and soon*
*   a lovely world smiles understandingly.*
Lightning is an essential part of God's plan for clearing
*   earth's atmosphere; likewise sorrow burns away*
*   the dross so that only lasting values remain.*
It is not finality. God is in control, using it in His
*   wonderful way for good.*[1]
— Carolyn Rhea

"Your mother might have two days to live. Her platelets are extremely low."

The oncologist reached me on my cell phone, and his words screeched more loudly than the brakes on the Chicago Metra train I was riding. This time there was no conference room I could run into to hide my tears. He explained the terminal condition known as Myelodysplastic Syndrome and described the unusually aggressive pace in which my mother's MDS was turning into Acute Myeloid Leukemia. My mother was dying. Grief once again had struck my life.

On the same day my dad died, lightning struck his beloved ficus tree on campus at Palm Beach Atlantic College and splintered it into a pile of twigs. Grief's inexplicable strike can devastate; yet God's grace can recycle our splintered lives.

In the preface of *When Grief Is Your Constant Companion,* my mother poignantly captures the shock of grief's unexpected strike.

A fierce storm lashed West Palm Beach during the pre-dawn hours of Wednesday, September 19, 1990. Startled by a brilliant flash of lightning followed almost instantly by house-shaking thunder, I awoke. For a long while I lay awake thinking, "What an awful storm! Lightning must have struck nearby. If only Claude were here." But my husband, Dr. Claude Rhea, couldn't be with me at this time. He was in Paris, France, on a business trip.

Later that day, I was chatting with a friend after I spoke at a luncheon at Palm Beach Atlantic College (now Palm Beach Atlantic University), where my husband was president.

"Carolyn, have you seen the tree that was struck by lightning early this morning?" she inquired.

"Which tree?" I asked. "One here on campus?"

"Yes, the huge ficus tree outside Claude's office."

Of course I wanted to see it! How Claude loved that tree! To him it was symbolic of Palm Beach Atlantic College. When he accepted the presidency of that college eight and one-half years earlier, the old ficus tree had stood valiantly among the old campus buildings. During Claude's time there, several new buildings were constructed. He had the majestic ficus tree dug up and transplanted (by crane!) just outside his office.

When my friend and I reached the site of the fallen tree, nothing remained. During the early morning storm, lightning had splintered its frame in an instant. Removing it quickly was imperative, for it had become a traffic hazard. Freshly placed flagstones created a virgin path across the ground so recently sheltered by Claude's beloved ficus tree. For a short while, my friend and I stood there talking about Claude's fallen tree.

Meanwhile, my husband, Claude, was waiting in Charles de Gaulle Airport near Paris, France for a flight to London. Suddenly, he experienced great difficulty breathing and was rushed to the emergency clinic at the airport. Doctors tried in vain to save his life. He died of heart failure there in the airport at 8:25 P.M. Paris time (2:25 P.M. West Palm Beach time).

The last words he spoke were these: "Tell Carolyn I love her."

My friend and I did not know that, while we were standing at the site of the fallen tree, my beloved husband of 39 years lay dying in France. Never again would his loving presence shelter me, his wife and helpmate. My life was changed forever. I was now a widow, wandering alone in the wilderness of grief.[2]

Due to the protocol of a death overseas, it took several days to have my dad's body flown back to Florida. My college French helped as I spoke with people in Paris and the American embassy to make arrangements. We met his casket at the airport. His luggage also arrived. My mother had unpacked a few important items from his garment bag. My mom had found tucked away in one of the garment bag's pockets a silk scarf. "I'm sure he must have bought this for you. He knew how much you loved silk scarves from France." It was a beautiful yellow and azure scarf. Perfect for springtime. Years ago, my dad had given me a pink Hermes scarf. He knew that I loved all things French, especially designer items. (As a teenager, I had traveled to Paris with my parents. Confident in my "fluency," I had gone to a hair salon. To this day, I don't know what I said, but I exited the place looking like Orphan Annie with very fluffy hair that took a few days to deflate.) I still wear these elegant French silk scarves on special occasions in honor of my dad.

Trying to clear any tangible reminders that might upset my mother, I took the garment bag to the garage area that had been turned into a large study. Alone, I pulled out his dress shirt and held it close to my cheeks. It still smelled like him. Old Lyme cologne. His favorite. My tears soaked through his cotton button-down.

The next few days were a complete blur. My brothers planned the memorial service, and Dave helped organize my dad's important papers. Meanwhile, I went with my mother to choose a casket. I can honestly say that was the worst shopping trip I ever had. We decided on a burnished copper finish. Then, we met with the same florist with whom we had just planned the wedding flowers. My mother and I decided that a large cascade of red roses and ivy would look beautiful for my dad. Each day, friends brought home-cooked meals for us. To maintain a sense of normalcy, we would eat dinner each evening at the dining room table. I will be forever grateful to those wonderful comforters who kept us nourished when we barely had an appetite.

People celebrated my father's life with two memorial services: one for the college students at Palm Beach Atlantic University where he was president, and the other for family and friends. First Baptist Church of West Palm Beach was packed at both services. My father was truly loved and admired by so many people. Music, laughter and tears filled the sanctuary. My oldest brother, Claude, found the strength to share the family's thoughts about my dad with the congregation. All I could do was bite back the tears and hold onto Dave's hand for strength. After the service, we had a private burial service. Each of us went home with a single red rose and sprig of ivy that covered his casket. That was a tangible reminder we could carry with us. The ivy could be planted and could continue growing, and the rose could be pressed. I must confess, as one that kills silk plants, my sprig of ivy didn't make it. But to have something tangible on the day of the funeral to carry home with me was a source of comfort.

After any kind of loss, family dynamics always seem to change. I was always a "daddy's girl." Mother-daughter relationships can be complicated. Ours was further compounded by my father's death and yes, my wedding. After my dad's death, my mother's life froze — like a computer that is stuck on one page. I ended up doing everything for the wedding on my own and with the help of some friends. One afternoon during my lunch break, I hailed a taxi from Wall Street and went to Kleinfeldt's in Brooklyn and chose my wedding dress. I selected the invitations and handled the announcements in the newspapers. I coordinated the menus, the venues and even the bridesmaids' shoes. With clarity of hindsight, I understand that my mother was in complete shock, unable to enjoy life and even the wedding of her only daughter. I wasn't angry at my mother, but I felt abandoned and unplugged. Ironically, my mother and I had started to connect over the details of the wedding prior to my father's death. She was the one I was calling from New York to ask for opinions on etiquette and plans. Then, on September 19, everything changed. She slipped into an abyss that only now can I fully understand.

My mother was buried on Good Friday. How fitting that she passed away during Holy Week. She was one of the most committed Christian women I had ever known. As one who accepted Christ into my life at a young age, I know that death is not the end, but rather the beginning. Because Christ died for us and was resurrected from the dead, we, too, can experience God's miraculous grace and spend eternity with Him.

Sure, death might not sting for those believers who pass away, but for those of us left behind those emotional hornets of guilt and regret certainly can swarm around and sting to the core. Loss is tragic. That is the reality.

After a loss, many people try to comfort us. The kind words are appreciated, but sometimes the truth is that people just don't say what we may need to hear. To be fair, people might not know exactly what should be said. A dear friend who lost an adult son told me,

BURIAL

My beloved is buried, Father.
His earthly body —
He whom I knew and loved so well —
Lies in the grave.
Forever beyond my mortal reach.

Never again will I rush into his arms.
And feel his warm embrace.
Or sit beside him and pour out my heart.
Or lie beside him and snuggle close.
Or worship with him and hear his songs of praise.
Or work with him in educating college students.
Or laugh with him at funny things
Enhanced by his wit.
Or cry with him when sorrow comes.
Or dine with him on food he lovingly prepared.
Or travel with him as citizens of God's world.
Or walk with him and talk along the way.
Or kneel with him and pray.

He is gone, Lord.
Death has claimed my love.

I stand at his grave and weep.
Are you here weeping with me, Lord?
Waiting to comfort me
When I reach out to You?

Please put your loving arms around me, Lord,
And hold me close.[3]
—CAROLYN RHEA

"You would not believe what some people have told me, thinking that they are comforting me. Someone should write a book about 'what not to say' to someone who has lost a loved one."

Finding the right words can be a challenge. But please don't ever say to anyone, "Well, at least you had your dad for 28 years." Believe me, those are not words of comfort. How can the measurement of time be applied to the measurement of one's grief? Quite honestly, I found the most comfort when friends would just call and say that they didn't know what to say but that they were here for me if I needed to talk or cry. In response to those that might not have said the most comforting words to me, I thanked them for their concern and for being there to support me. Being there — whether in person, by phone, by letter — provides comfort.

As my mother writes in *When Grief Is Your Constant Companion*, the one in whom we will find real comfort is the Holy Spirit.

Recently, my parents' final items in storage arrived at my front doorstep. Inside these cardboard boxes I discovered spiritual gems — my mother's Bible, devotional books she had read on a daily basis, her journals, love letters from my dad to my mother, letters from my grandmothers and my grandfather along with many other treasures. What an awakening it has been to read my mother's notes in the margins of her Bible along with highlighted passages. In a sense, I have almost felt like a trespasser, reading personal excerpts from her life's journey that she never fully discussed with me. Yet, I realize now that these moments of joy, doubt and trust were meant to be read and shared. They were left as guiding footprints of faith. This path has not only led me to a closer relationship with God, but also to a place of comfort where I now have a deeper understanding of and love for my mother. I pray that you too will find comfort from the many words my mother wrote — many that were published, but some that were privately marked within the margins. I pray that this book will increase your faith and remind you that our hope is in Christ.

My Comforters

I understand more about Job's comforters now, Lord,
For I have had comforters, too.

Family came.
We opened our arms to each other
And grieved at our loss,
Shared memories that would bless
And love that could help heal.

Friends came.
Some to weep with me,
Saying not a word
But surrounding me with love.
Some to embrace me in my grief
And tell me that they care.
Some to say "I know exactly how you feel."
(How can they truly know?)
And some to preach to me,
Telling me to be brave and not cry,
To trust and not doubt.
Some comforters help bear my burden.
Others added to it.
I know every comforter's intent was good, Father,
And I'm grateful for everyone who cared enough
To come, to call, to write.

And then the Holy Spirit came,
The true Comforter whom You sent, Lord Jesus,
To anchor my life in Your love and truth
At this turbulent time
And to call to remembrance Your words
That I need to hear.
The Holy Presence — Calming my troubled spirit
And consoling my broken heart.[4]
— Carolyn Rhea

Comfort

"Daughter, be of good comfort." Matthew 9:22

"I will not leave you comfortless: I will come to you." John 14:18

"The Lord is nigh unto them that are of a broken heart."
Psalm 34:18

"Blessed are they that mourn: for they shall be comforted." Matthew 5:4

"The Spirit of the Lord GOD is upon me . . . .he hath sent me to bind up the brokenhearted . . . to comfort all that mourn . . . to give unto them beauty for ashes, the oil of joy for mourning." Isaiah 61:1–3

"Be strong in the grace that is in Christ Jesus." 2 Timothy 2:1

"For we walk by faith, not by sight." 2 Corinthians 5:7

"Eye hath not seen, nor ear heard . . . the things which God hath prepared for them that love him." 1 Corinthians 2:9

"I will make thee . . . a joy of many generations." Isaiah 60:15

"Death is swallowed up in victory. O death, where is thy sting? O grave, where is thy victory? . . . But thanks be to God which giveth us the victory through our Lord Jesus Christ." 1 Corinthians 15:54–55, 57

Counsel

- Simply being with someone who is grieving is a huge source of support — holding space and letting them know you just want to be with them. They must know that they do not have to take care of you. You will be there to support them in any way they want, whether it be talking, listening or just hanging out.

Rich Blue, M.A., LCPC, IBCC, NCC, founder of Center for Christian Life Enrichment and clinical director, is a licensed clinical professional counselor with more than 25 years of experience.

- Because people are in shock, they do not think as clearly, so it's not helpful if friends and family overload them with theological treatises on the meaning of suffering and death. Job's friends sat in silence with him for a week, which was a comforting thing to do. Then they opened their mouths and the trouble started! Listening is so much better than talking. If you don't know the answer to a question (such as "Why did God allow my loved one to die?"), then say, "I don't know." Give people space to get angry at God, at the dead person, etc. Don't try to talk them out of their feelings or say, "You shouldn't feel that way." Friends and family can help by taking care of daily tasks that can seem overwhelming to the grieving person, such as mowing the lawn, laundry, preparing a meal. For more sensitive tasks, such as packing away the deceased person's clothing, it's always best to offer your help rather than just jumping in and taking on that task yourself. Don't say to a grieving person, "God needed your loved one and that's why He took him/her to heaven," or, "It was a blessing that s/he died." If the grieving person says, "it was a blessing that s/he died," you can nod and smile, but don't be the first one to offer that interpretation of what happened.

  In the months and years to come, do mention periodically that you miss someone's deceased loved one. Often, the grieving wonder if anyone remembers their loved one. It can be such a blessing to have someone come up and mention your loved one or tell you a funny or sweet story about your loved one.

Jennifer Degler, PhD is a clinical psychologist, life coach and coauthor of No More Christian Nice Girl: How Just Being Nice — Instead of Good — Hurts You, Your Family, and Your Friends.

- I think the best approach is to give someone who experiences loss very wide latitude. They will at times express outrageous conclusions, anger, blame. The natural response for the friend and counselor is to refute false statements and try to simmer down some of the rage, but I think that's a mistake. I think you just need to be there, comfort, love, pray, and most importantly, seek concrete ways to meet their physical needs. Your presence is the most important thing you can give. And if you have good times, words of comfort, Scripture verses that heal, and just the ability to enter into their sorrow and weep with them. One thing I have learned in the past few years is that sometimes the most important thing you can do to help a person grieving is meet their physical needs. Often someone in grief neglects their nourishment, their care of their bodies, and they need a stable friend to help manage this in a gentle way. Meals delivered. Clean laundry. Rides to and from important appointments. Paying bills. Those all sound so pedestrian and unspiritual, but they are honestly some of the greatest gifts you can give a person suffering loss.

I'm reminded of God's response to Elijah, who in 1 Kings 19 was in the throes of severe despondency. God's immediate reaction wasn't some deep spiritual insight, but to give Elijah not one, but two meals. In the midst of his trial, he had forgotten to take care of his body. I can't stress enough how important it is to take care of the physical and then proceed with the spiritual, and when the spiritual applications begin to take hold, begin and end with hope. You need to infuse your friend with the hope of Jesus Christ, with the sovereignty of God, and the knowledge that life will begin to get good again.

Daniel Darling is senior pastor of Gages Lake Bible Church in the northwest suburbs of Chicago. Daniel is the author of Teen People of the Bible, Crash Course, *and* iFaith.

CHRONICLING

(Dear Reader, this is your section for your story. Your feelings. Your grief. Use this as a journal to record your journey through the loss. The questions are some guidelines, but don't have to be answered.)

Where was I and what happened when my loss occurred?

Who have my "comforters" been?

What comforts me the most during difficult days?

What did someone say or write that provided great comfort?

What do I want to say to God right now? Here is my letter to Him:

Dear God,

Denial ··· Denial ··· Denial

Chapter 3

My heart listens for your return, my love.
I hear a plane overhead and think that you're flying home from
    Europe.
I hear a car in the driveway and believe that you're back!
I'm ready to rush to the door to welcome you
And hear your glad words: "I'm home, darling!"
But you are not there.
I am the one to open the door each time
And say to an empty house, "I'm home, darling!
In the store, I find myself still planning meals
For both of us
Or buying your favorite foods instead of mine.
And sometimes while I'm cooking dinner,
My heart hears you drive up outside.
It's only a daydream.
I must dine alone.
Perhaps if you had not been
Overseas when you died,
There would be no such fantasies.
My mind knows that I shall go to you.

I remember
the time I flew alone to Amsterdam
To join you for the choir tour.
"What if he isn't there to meet me?
How will I make connections? I'm scared!"
I needn't have worried at all.
You were there, my love, waiting for me,
Waving your arms joyously,
And shouting, "Welcome, darling!"
You have gone ahead, my love.
And I shall join you there!
My heart anticipates your glad shout:
"Welcome, darling!" [1]
—— CAROLYN RHEA

"May I please have your permission to die?"

My mother's voice was weak, yet the strength of her question still pierces my heart. It was almost midnight when the phone rang. The caregiver had called 911. The paramedics spoke with me on the phone and explained that my mother refused to go to the emergency room. I immediately phoned my oldest brother, Claude, to conference him in so he could be part of this very difficult conversation. I couldn't handle this alone, and my oldest brother was already scheduled to head to Florida in the morning.

Denial is a surreal state of mind. It's as if someone is at your front door pressing the doorbell, but you don't hear any sound. And since you don't hear any sound, you convince yourself that maybe no one is actually there. Denial is a protective disconnection that delays acknowledgement of what is real and too painful to encounter.

I knew my mother was physically exhausted from the incessant transfusions and the alternative medicine. She could no longer tolerate food and constantly talked in her sleep as if she were having conversations with people I couldn't see. I knew my mother was ready to die and go home to heaven, but I wasn't ready for her to leave. That night on the phone, she asked for permission to die. She wanted me to let her go, but I couldn't let her go. One of my greatest regrets in life is that I didn't say the words that my mother so desperately wanted to hear that night: "Yes. You've finished the race, Mother. Go to God. Give Daddy a hug. I love you." Instead, I chose to deny her imminent death and instead pleaded with my mother, "Please just go to the hospital with the paramedics and you will feel better, OK? I don't want you to die. I love you."

That night, I couldn't sleep. My mother had asked my permission to die, and I had denied what would be her final request. She had fought courageously against this disease for almost four months. She was exhausted, and I had forced her to go to the hospital with the paramedics to face yet another round of transfusions.

Months later, my brother, Claude, received a letter from one of my mother's neighbors in Vero Beach. She wrote to thank him for sending a copy of the CD from Mother's funeral. She and many others were unable to travel to West Palm Beach for the service. In her letter, my mother's neighbor shared a story with my brother about how she ended up in the hospital after falling. Her words brought much comfort to me and also provide an insight into denial.

As I was sitting there waiting in the waiting room to see the doctor, the two paramedics that brought me began inquiring about your mother and how she was and what had happened to her. Of course I told them that she had passed on. They were so very sorry and began talking about what a wonderful person she was. I began to cry and they were sorry they had made me cry. I was glad because I had shed no tears for Carolyn and had thought about it and had decided it was because I had not been able to go to her funeral. Even though I have missed her so much and thought about her often and looked over at her place thinking she is not there anymore and how I longed to see her, I had still not shed a tear. All of a sudden as we were talking with the paramedics about her and I was crying and they were lamenting that they had made me cry. . . . I just seemed to feel her near. . . . I thanked the paramedics for asking about her. I was thankful that I had finally cried. She had really made an impression on them.

This neighbor's letter helped assuage my guilt about forcing my mother to leave with the paramedics. Even as she inched closer to death, my mother's life still ripened with the fruits of God's spirit: goodness, love, kindness, gentleness, patience, peace, joy, self-control and faithfulness. As a result, she made a lasting impression on the lives of two paramedics.

Loss can feel like a nightmare, right? When I first heard about my mother's diagnosis of a terminal illness, I kept trying to wake up, but I was stuck in the shadows of my frightening dream. My mind knew the truth, but my heart still hoped that the pending death of my mother was not real. I resolved to find a cure and even contacted a top Chicago oncologist in the field of blood cancer to have a conference call with my mother's doctor in Florida. I convinced my mother to pursue an alternative treatment with controversial medicine that studies indicated would help. I was ready to fight and wanted her to fight, too. Surely the pebble in my slingshot would kill the giant called Leukemia. Of course I had prayed to God, but I had not surrendered in full this life-and-death crisis to Him. Instead, I prayed, aimed and fired. My years in New York City banking had trained me well to don the necessary armor to get the job done, expeditiously and effectively. A strategic plan was in place. Doctors were in agreement. I was armed for battle, and determination was my weapon of choice. But peace was nowhere in sight.

With the perspective of years, I sometimes wonder if my denial were partially a denial of the sufficiency of the presence of God's grace. Even though Jesus was with the disciples on the boat as the turbulent waves crashed against the vessel, the disciples still panicked. The mere presence of the Holy One wasn't sufficient for these frightened men. They demanded His physical presence to encounter the storm and prevent everyone from drowning. "And his disciples came to him, and awoke him, saying, Lord, save us: we perish. And he saith unto them, Why are ye fearful, O ye of little faith? Then he arose, and rebuked the winds and the sea; and there was a great calm" (Matthew 8:25–26). I panicked when the doctor told me that my mother might only live for two days. My vessel was shaken to the core. I needed to hold tightly onto something tangible. My knowledge of God's presence of grace was somehow not sufficient for me at that moment of battling the storm. Like the disciples, I, too, needed Him to just show up and personally say, "Peace. Be still."

In hindsight, I should have chosen instead to "let go and let grow" (my own twist to the adage "let go and let God"). Please note that I am not saying, "Surrender to death." Instead, I am saying, "Surrender to God." It's only by letting go that something can grow. As a young child I remember squeezing the large bud of an orange daylily along the side of our driveway in Alabama. "Mother, why didn't the pretty flower pop out?" I had asked, thinking that I was helping the daylily bloom. She gently touched my shoulders and said, "You can't make something bloom before it is time."

One of my mother's notes in the margins of her Bible says, "Forsaking All I Trust Him." The letting go process is the foundation of faith. On the side margin of that same page in her Bible, my mother wrote "from complaint and questioning to trust and praise." That is the outgrowth of faith.

My father's life embodied faith in the Lord. As an encourager, he always insisted that faith should be an action verb and not a noun. "Faith God," he would say. At age 30, my dad was diagnosed with cancer of the cecum, a type of colon cancer. I was not yet born. In fact, it is a true miracle that I am even here on Earth. In the 1950s there were no options for radiation or chemotherapy.

Reading from my dad's autobiography, *With My Song I Will Praise Him*, I was struck by the candor with which he shared his diagnosis and the ensuing denial of facing his own death.

"This white spot about the size of a crabapple in your right side is the cancer," he (the doctor) said. "It's on the cecum. These streaks seem to indicate that it's metastasized, that is, spread. It doesn't look good at all. You'll need immediate surgery — tomorrow! I suggest you choose a surgeon right now. Any questions?"

Questions? Questions? How could I frame questions in a mind that was gripped by the icy reality of the words I had just heard from the doctor? I was shattered. Incredulous. Unnerved. Aghast. Unbelieving. I arranged for a surgeon and then, trance-like moved from the cool antiseptic climate of the doctor's office out into a bright autumn afternoon . . .

How could I tell my wife Carolyn and our children the news? How does a man share his deepest agony with his dearest ones? Slowly I climbed from the car and went toward them. My family was raking leaves. The beautiful scene burned itself deeply into my memory. Joyous family togetherness. My children frolicked in piles of raked-up tree-abandoned leaves, throwing them like lazy, weightless javelins at nonexistent enemies.

Carolyn looked up, caught my eye, and read my plight even before I could utter a word. With the sixth sense of a wife, she already seemed to know. Wordlessly, she came to me and hand-in-hand, we slipped quietly into our bedroom. Closing the door, we fell to our knees, crying our hearts out to God. At that moment in time, I felt as Elijah must have felt in that long ago. . . . Abandoned . . . stricken . . . "the heavens were as brass." Prayers seemed to stop at the ceiling.[2]

I was surprised at first to read in print those words penned by my father who always overflowed with faith and optimism about God's plan and purpose. My heart ached that he had felt abandoned by God. How was it even possible that my mother — the epitome of a prayer warrior — ever felt that God wasn't listening to her prayers?

As an adult, I can now read these words and better understand my parents' sense of despair during that crisis. My mother probably trembled at the thought of being a young widow and raising two young sons without her loving husband. In addition to the sheer physical pain he would face with surgery, my father probably also worried about leaving loved ones behind. My dad also relinquished his life dream of becoming an overseas missionary. My parents had planned to make this decision public the following week. My father picked up the phone and called Dr. Baker James Cauthen, executive secretary of the Foreign Mission Board to share the grim news. He writes about that conversation in his book.

"Will you pray for us, Dr. Cauthen?" I requested.

This gracious, powerful man of God quietly and simply said, "Yes, Claude, I will." It was only months later that I learned the extent of his simple pledge to me. For immediately he cabled missionary "prayer warriors" around the world. Within a matter of hours there was a far-flung intercessory prayer meeting going on — one that encircled the entire globe.

I slept fitfully that night, tossing and turning, mulling over the traumatic events of the day, consciously and subliminally experiencing agonies both real and imagined. Mercifully, sleep came in the early morning grayness.

When I awoke to a new day, there was a different dimension. Something was happening. I was experiencing a new process. I was on the receiving end of intercessory prayer! My wife, Carolyn, captured the essence of this moment in a poem from one of her books, My Heart Kneels Too.

The Invisible Seesaw

I felt that someone prayed for me,
For there came an inner awareness
That someone cared enough to send through God
Remembrance of my heavy burden and my special need of Him.
It was as if God's mercy
Transformed that prayer into an invisible seesaw
Which lifted me while the weight of my burden
Rested briefly on the other end.
And with the lightened load, my tenseness thawed in the
warm therapy of love and care
And new strength came now that I was more relaxed and trusting.
I knew that somewhere someone had prayed for me.

Yes, intercessory prayer, the invisible seesaw, made the difference. The new antiseptic world of the hospital didn't seem quite as formidable and impersonal. The unknown and as yet uncharted map of oncoming pain seemed somehow to be definable and bearable.[3]

Months later, after an arduous and miraculous recovery from his cancer surgery, my father found out how well Dr. Cauthen had kept his promise. He had cabled missionary "prayer warriors" around the world, and within a matter of hours, a global intercessory prayer meeting had taken place. There was no trace of the cancerous growth anywhere in his body. Even the doctors couldn't explain what had happened. My father knew. He was the recipient of an unexpected grace gift from God. As my dad writes in his book, "Prayer precipitated a twentieth-century miracle in my body. God in his mercy heard and answered — and healed!"[4]

God doesn't tune out the cries of His children. He does not wear earplugs. As Jeremiah 33:3 reminds us, "Call unto me, and I will answer thee, and shew thee great and mighty things which thou knowest not." However, the decibel level of denial within the cacophony of grief is what prevents us from hearing God's still, small voice that says, "And thine ears shall hear a word behind thee, saying, This is the way, walk ye in it, when ye turn to the right hand, and when ye turn to the left" (Isaiah 30:21).

In my mother's case, God heard, but He didn't heal. My mother whispered her final words to me on the phone that night after I refused to give her permission to die: "I love you." She slipped into a coma the next day at the hospital, and I scrambled to find a flight to Florida. She waited for all three children to be gathered in her hospital room holding hands around her bed while my oldest brother read Psalm 23. "And though I walk through the valley of the shadow of death, I will fear not . . ." After nearly a four-month battle against an aggressive form of leukemia, Mother took her final breath at 8:25 P.M. — the same time my father had died many years before in Paris.

Even though my mother was dead, I still held onto her hand. I couldn't let her go. This was my final act of denial. I kept waiting for her to squeeze my hand three times with our secret message of "I love you." But her hand was still. She was no longer there. At age 41, I felt like an abandoned child in desperate need of a mother's reaffirming love. Even to this day, I have kept two of my mother's voice messages on my answering machine. On those really difficult days, I call voice mail and listen to her gentle Southern accent in which she reminds me at the end of each message, "I love you."

I squeezed my mother's hand one last time with our secret signal of "I love you," then I gently released her to heaven. I let go and let grow. It was her time to bloom in heaven, and it was my time to grow deeper roots of faith as I took my own journey of grief.

Although faith is our GPS, the journey can be subject to many emotional detours, especially when we encounter delayed intensity of feelings, and that's OK. I need to insert a confession here. In writing this book, I realized that there were still some lingering emotions of denial that manifested itself through procrastination of this project. "Oh, I'll work on the book next week. I have family visiting from out of town," I would convince myself. The truth is, each time I sat at my desk with the computer and began reading the letters and writings of my parents, my aunt and grandfather, I would sob. The emotions were surprisingly still raw. Please know that there is no statute of limitation on how long one can grieve over a loss. Each one of us has our own timetable and an individual journey to take in order to reach an ultimate place of acceptance and understanding that God's grace truly is sufficient.

Comfort

"And as Jesus passed by, he saw a man which was blind from his birth. And his disciples asked him saying, Master, who did sin, this man, or his parents, that he was born blind? Jesus answered, Neither hath this man sinned, nor his parents: but that the works of God should be made manifest in him." John 9:1–3

"Though he slay me, yet will I trust in him." Job 13:15

"The righteous perish . . . devout [men] are taken away, and no one understands that the righteous are taken away to be spared from evil." Isaiah 57:1 (NIV)

"For now we see through a glass, darkly, but then face to face: now I know in part; but then shall I know even as also I am known." 1 Corinthians 13:12

"Put thou my tears into thy bottle: are they not in thy book?" Psalm 56:8

"For thou art my hope, O Lord GOD: thou art my trust from my youth." Psalm 71:5

"Hear my prayer, O LORD, and give ear unto my cry; hold not thy peace at my tears." Psalm 39:12

"Come unto me, all ye that labor and are heavy laden, and I will give you rest." MATTHEW 11:28

"Rest in the Lord, and wait patiently for him." PSALM 37:7

"And God shall wipe away all tears from their eyes." REVELATION 7:17

"Peace I leave with you, my peace I give unto you: not as the world giveth, give I unto you. Let not your heart be troubled, neither let it be afraid." JOHN 14:27

COUNSEL

- The answers to "Why?" will not release us from the pain. The real question isn't "why." The truth of the question is we're wrestling with the trustworthiness of God. We pin all bad things on God because He's sovereign. Why didn't He stop this bad thing from happening? Is God trustworthy when He allows bad times to come into our lives? We do mental gymnastics with who God is. We need to get to know who God really is and allow Him into our pain and present. We must build a relationship with God. There will be times of woundedness. For three years after the death of my mother, I kept God at a distance. But there came a time for me to give it up to God — the anger, bitterness and hurt. It's about a life of surrender. *Ray Ercoli, former director of programs and workshops at Willow Creek Community Church*

- Denial is normal and natural. It is a stage people move in and out of. It helps to understand when someone is in denial and gently remind them that they are probably still experiencing some sense of shock in response to the loss. They are not able yet to fully process the impact of the loss. Their unconscious is allowing them to experience the losses in stages. Again, getting through in most cases is just a matter of being with someone and letting them gradually adjust and accept reality. I think of it like letting feeling come back to your foot after it has "fallen asleep." *Rich Blue*

- This first stage of grieving helps us to survive the loss. In this stage, the world becomes meaningless and overwhelming. Life makes no sense. We are in a state of shock and denial. We go numb. We wonder how we can go on, if we can go on, why we should go on. We try to find a way to simply get through each day. Denial and shock help us to cope and make survival possible. Denial helps us to pace our feelings of grief. There is a grace in denial. It is nature's way of letting in only as much as we can handle. On Grief and Grieving: Finding the Meaning of Grief Through the Five Stages of Loss, *by Elisabeth Kübler-Ross, M.D., David Kessler*

CHRONICLING

What do I need to surrender to God right now?

How has my faith been impacted as a result of what happened?

Am I fully connected to my emotions, or am I still keeping them at a distance?

What else do I need to say to God?

43

Dear God,

Chapter 4

Anger ··· Anger ··· Anger

Anger boils within me as steaming water in a kettle.
Scalding words thrown indiscriminately upon the innocent as
well as upon the offender will scald and scar.
Through self control, I must keep anger contained within the
kettle so that its blistering steam does not injure.[1]
— CAROLYN RHEA

"Mother, I'm so sorry I can't fly to Florida. I broke my elbow and have to have surgery tomorrow."

On March 13, 2003 — merely a month before my mother died — I slipped on black ice while taking the garbage can to the curb. It is one of the late-winter challenges of living in a Chicago suburb. Thankfully, the garbage can prevented me from falling on my head, but I broke my left elbow. The next day I underwent surgery and had three pins inserted into my elbow to hold it together. I couldn't physically manage to visit my dying mother for another two and a-half weeks. I was angry at myself and at the circumstances. We talked on the phone, however, and my mother shared her own experience about breaking her elbow when my older brothers were young children. They had splashed water from the bath onto the floor, and my mom slipped on the tile and also had to have pins surgically inserted. My mother wanted to help take care of me, and I wanted to help take care of her. At last when I could travel, I wasn't much of a help to my mother or to the caregiver. I was frustrated that I couldn't even drive my mother to her doctor's appointment for a transfusion, but at least I was there. We spent hours together in the family room and talked.

My mother's writings about anger surprised me. Quite honestly, I never saw her express explosive anger. Instead, she packaged her anger in creative and productive ways.

As a young child I suffered from a benign kidney problem, and my mother had to take me to see the urologist quite often. These visits were during the days when smoking was allowed in doctors' offices. Extremely allergic, my mother despised being around secondhand smoke. I will never forget how angry my mother looked when a smoker was reading a magazine next to her, and the cigarette smoke wafted directly into my mother's face. Instead of confronting the person, my mother picked up a thick magazine and waved the fog of smoke back to the smoker. Without even an exchange of words, the person quickly extinguished the cigarette, and we enjoyed a smoke-free wait in the office.

As a busy young teen, I constantly kept my room in complete disarray, and that made my mom angry. However, she didn't confront me by yelling; instead, she wrote me a long letter about how upsetting it was that I kept my room messy when she and my dad worked so hard to provide such lovely clothes and items for me.

With her relatively mild approach to anger, you can imagine my shock when I read this next passage that my mother wrote in her book about grief.

I'm Angry, Father!
I'm angry, Father!
Angry at YOU for taking
My beloved from me,
Angry at LIFE for
Crippling me so,
Angry at my BELOVED for
Dying and leaving me,
Angry at MYSELF for
Being angry!

I'm angry
That my dear husband isn't here to help me.
(I was always there to help him.)
Angry that he didn't take better care of himself.
Angry that he didn't see a doctor sooner.
Angry that he didn't slow down and have us
Do the things we'd planned together.

Lord, how can I possibly be mad at my beloved?

Death was not his choosing.
He loved me and wanted to live.
He was just too busy doing Your work, Father,
And loved doing it!
Always, he put others' needs before his own.
Neglecting himself
But never neglecting others.
He trusted Your will in all things.

So why should I lash out at You, Father,
When I know Your will is truly best
And that his love for me
Was a special gift from You?

Is anger a natural part of grief?
Must it be acknowledged and expressed
Before healing can come?

Let anger dissipate, Lord,
And Your peace flow in to take its place.[2]
— CAROLYN RHEA

In the preface of C. S. Lewis's book *A Grief Observed*, Madeleine L'Engle writes:

I am grateful, too, to Lewis for having the courage to yell, to doubt, to kick at God with angry violence. This is a part of healthy grief not often encouraged. It is helpful indeed that C. S. Lewis, who has been such a successful apologist for Christianity, should have the courage to admit doubt about what he has so superbly proclaimed. It gives us permission to admit our own doubts, our own angers and anguishes, and to know that they are part of the soul's growth.[3]

Anger is indeed a natural part of grief. For some people, anger reconnects the wiring of the "denial doorbell." Sometimes anger can appear when least expected, prompted by a submerged catalyst. After becoming an adult orphan, I wasn't "angry" at God. Sure, I was deeply resentful that my father couldn't be the one to walk me down the aisle on my wedding day and that my mother couldn't be here for all the milestones of my family. Future events prompted by a submerged catalyst, however, would ignite my anger.

The day after Thanksgiving in 1996, I was in a horrible car accident. Thankfully, my children were at home with Dave, who had taken an extra day off from work. I was returning home from the grocery store when a truck carrying 3,000 pounds of ice cream toppled on its side and careened across two lanes of traffic onto my car. My station wagon ended up in a ditch with smoke pouring from the truck into the driver's side, and the back of the car wrapped around a tree. The impact somehow knocked me to the passenger's side with my seatbelt intact, and I opened my eyes to this frightening scene. A "Good Samaritan" helped me crawl out of the car through the passenger window since the doors wouldn't open. The fire chief who inspected the accident told me that it was a miracle I hadn't been killed. God's grace was truly present.

After the moment of impact, however, I had a calm peace even though I was trapped in that car. Although I didn't hear an audible voice, my mind heard my father's gentle voice say, "It's not your time. Everything will be OK." Only later did the anger come. No bones were broken, but my twisted back was in great pain. A mom doesn't get sick days, and I had two little girls to care for. I resented the emotional and physical pain that this accident caused. I couldn't pick up my children and play with them in the backyard for several weeks. And we lost money in replacing the totaled car with a new one. Even though I was physically healing, I was still an emotional wreck. I am convinced that the intensity of my anger was my delayed emotional grief over losing my dad. At last that "doorbell of denial" connected, and my emotions exploded. For the next few weeks, I constantly sobbed in the shower.

Just recently did anger surface its ugly head again in a delayed reaction to my mother's passing. As a mom trying to balance family, home, work and life, I felt overwhelmed. I resented not being able to pick up the phone and talk to my mother either for parenting advice, or for that certain ingredient in a dish or even to read my latest chapter aloud to her on the phone. At that moment, I felt simultaneously the fullness and the emptiness of being an adult orphan. So I did what I typically do when I need a good cry. I took a shower and sobbed, allowing the water to mute my tears. It was during Mother's Day week that I at last dreamed about her. Just like my mother who wasn't able to dream about my dad until several years after he died, I, too, wasn't able to dream about her until days before Mother's Day. In that dream, she and my dad were enjoying a celebration in heaven. She smiled at me and said, "Just be patient. Everything will be OK."

In the last box of my mother's items I found heavily worn and underlined copies of *Streams in the Desert* and *My Utmost for His Highest.* What a joyful surprise to discover my grandmother's signature on the front page of *Streams in the Desert* dated 1950. Beneath my grandmother's formal signature, Mrs. Boyd Turnage, my mother signed her name: Carolyn Turnage Rhea. In 2010, I signed my name beneath my mother's signature: Margaret Rhea McSweeney. Three generations of women united and comforted over a period of 60 years.

I noticed that in the left margin of the April 19 devotion in *Streams in the Desert,* my mother wrote this note: "Dream of Mother — trying to help me with my schedule and destination." My mother, too, had a dream about her own mother during a difficult time — most likely when she was trying to decide where to live and what to do after my dad died. Underlined in green marker were the words: "In times of uncertainty, wait." Essentially, the same message: "Just be patient." But sometimes anger and faith seem completely incompatible. But are they? Anger screams for an answer to the interminable question of "Why?"

Even Jesus experienced this anguish on the Cross. "And at the ninth hour Jesus cried out in a loud voice, *'Eloi, Eloi, lama sabachthani?'* which means, 'My God, my God, why have you forsaken me?'" (Mark 15:34). The Son of God felt abandonment and despair, but He knew that His Father was faithful. Anger is a human emotion. Faith, however, is the spiritual connection that helps smooth the disheveled life after loss. And peace is the ultimate outcome of our faith through God's grace.

Quite honestly, the journey to "peace" is not an easy one, at least it hasn't been for me, nor was it for my mother. Life is not a "yellow brick road" but rather one that has huge potholes, detours, and sometimes even unexpected tragedy. Although faith is our GPS and we diligently obey God's "rules of the road," why do horrible things still happen? Is that really God's will?

My mother agonized over this same concept, not only when my father died, but also when her only sister and sibling died at the age of 22 on August 1, 1948. I am named after my Aunt Margaret. She became a summer missionary on a reservation in Oklahoma after graduating from college at Florida State University. Recently, I found Aunt Margaret's final letters that she had written to my mother and my grandparents during the summer of 1948. Tears streamed down my face when I saw the birthday card to my mother for her 21st birthday. How young my mother was to lose a sister. They were roommates in college and best friends, too. How eerie to read Aunt Margaret's handwritten letter, an odd foreshadow to what would soon happen in her life. She wrote:

"Nothing too exciting has happened around here since I wrote you last. _______________ , an Indian about 26 years old (It's unnecessary to share his name) took me and Dot on a tour of the city in his new yellow convertible. We saw some sailboats and made some pictures of them as background. _______________ is a fine Christian man and gentleman and a very careful driver. We are very very careful with whom we ride so please don't worry about that."

Only weeks later, this young man fell asleep behind the wheel, and the convertible flipped over and killed Margaret.

After Margaret's death, my mother had the temerity to actually question the will of God. After my mother died, my oldest brother found a recording of a speech she had made at a church during the 1970s. I was shocked to hear her gentle Southern voice dare to directly question God's will. This was not the mother I knew, the reserved woman who always awoke at five in the morning to read her Bible and pray. Her words have given me permission to have an interactive and honest relationship with God. It's OK to question Him and to ask "Why?" These are my mother's words:

Thy Will Be Done?

The most the average Christian can hope to do is to take hold of the near edge of a great problem and act at some cost to himself — touching our world, our priority.

Many years ago my sister, Margaret, 22 years of age at the time, was killed in an automobile accident. She just graduated from Florida State University and was serving as a summer missionary to the Native American Indians in Oklahoma before attending seminary that fall to prepare herself to go as a missionary to China. Her life ended abruptly one week before her home mission work was completed.

At my parents' request, these words were carved on her tombstone, "Thy will be done." Somehow they helped assuage my parents' grief, but these words stirred up angry feelings in me. 1 asked God, "Is this the way you reward someone who loves you and serves you? Did you really care about Margaret's life? How can 1 ever pray and mean it, 'Thy will be done in my life too?'"

1 had to make peace with the will of God. Somehow 1 couldn't see the forest from the trees. On a personal basis, 1 can now welcome God's will into my own life for 1 believe that he wants me to grow toward spiritual maturity in Jesus Christ. He wants me to grow toward becoming my finest self, and 1 can grow only in the power of a personal faith relationship with Jesus. And as 1 grow, God wants me to reach out and bring others to him that they too might grow in Christ. You know within this larger context of the will of God, no human circumstance or tragic event is ever beyond the redemptive power of God. As 1 expectantly abide in God's ongoing will, he can work creatively for good in every situation and help me keep on growing as 1 reach up to him and out to others.

At the time of my sister's death, someone gave me a copy of Leslie Weatherhead's book, The Will of God. He presents three aspects of the will of God. First, the intentional will of God — that is His ideal plan for man. Second, the circumstantial will of God — God's plan within certain circumstances. And third, the ultimate will of God — His final realization of His purposes.

God's intentional or ideal will for Margaret, that she serve him by serving her fellow man as a missionary while she herself continued to grow in Christ, had been thwarted by the human circumstances of the driver's losing control of the car in which she was riding. Even then God could have miraculously spared her life, but being a Christian missionary did not automatically exempt Margaret from God's physical laws. Mercifully God took her home within the context of his circumstantial will. God's intentional, or ideal will had been thwarted, but His circumstantial will, I believe, was accomplished. God's ultimate will, his final realization of his purposes in Margaret's life that she be a blessing and influence for many lives for Christ triumphed even in her untimely death, for her life continues to bear fruit today.

Honorary pallbearers at her funeral service were members of the Margaret Turnage Life Service Band named in her honor. While earning her way through college as secretary in a local Baptist church, she had organized a group of some 36 young people and college students who met regularly to pursue God's will in their vocation. As my sister's college roommate, I had heard her pray often by name for each one of them. From that group have come many dedicated Christian leaders scattered around the world, all profoundly influenced by her life. And needless to say, her life left rich deposits in my life, too.

I learned the sequel to the story only recently. The driver who had lost control of the car in which my sister was killed was a young Indian. He was deeply affected by Margaret's life and her death. As a result, he opened up his own life for the will of God. For many years now he has been faithful in serving as a Baptist pastor to the Indians in Oklahoma.

The spiritual quality of Margaret's personhood in Jesus Christ was a dynamic force that God used creatively for good in the lives of many people. As Margaret grew towards spiritual maturity in Jesus Christ she reached out and brought others to Christ that they too might grow in him.

Touching the near edges of her immediate world for Jesus Christ was her priority. And in so doing, she continues to touch the far edges, too.

The most the average Christian can hope to do is to take hold of the near edge of a great problem and act at some cost to himself.

After my father died, my mother once again questioned God's will. She couldn't find an acceptable answer to "Why?" and searched for reasons why God took my dad home to heaven. The following poem is an outpouring of my mother's grief.

Why, Father? Why?
Why, Father? Why?
Why did You take my beloved from me?

Was it to punish me
With loneliness and grief?
For sins I have committed?
Losing him was life's greatest loss.
How could you hurt me so cruelly?
If his death were truly Your way of chastening me,
Then You are only to be feared, Father,
Not loved and trusted.
I have loved and trusted You
These many years
And my heart tells me
His death was not Your means
Of punishing me.
So I shall love and trust You still.
But why, Father? Why?
I do not understand.
Neither did my beloved.
Dying, he said,
"The Father wants me.

I do not understand.
There's so much more to do.
Tell Carolyn I love her."
And he died, serenely trusting You in death
Even as he had trusted You in life.
Was his earthly future bleak
With pain and helplessness?
Was death his highest good?
Was his work for You completed?
Did You, in love, call him home?
Your reasons are shrouded in mystery, Father.
But I trust you still.
Someday I'll understand.[4]
— CAROLYN RHEA

While leading a grief group in a church a few years ago, I met a father who was struggling for answers. His precious daughter had been murdered. Why would God allow such violence against innocence? I told him that I didn't know the answer to "Why?" And I couldn't even imagine the extreme pain that the father was experiencing after such a tragic loss. All I could do was to reach out to him as someone who had also lost a loved one and to let him know how much I cared and that I would pray for him and his family

This father looked at me and said, "Thank you for being honest. Most people try to come up with some kind of answer. And nothing makes sense."

Years later, I still long for words with which I could have better comforted this grieving father, but at that time I didn't personally know anyone else who had experienced such a shocking and violent death of an adult child. While having lunch recently with a friend, I mentioned the conversation with this man and how inadequate I still felt about my response. My friend graciously responded with a gentle reminder that Mary, the mother of our Lord and Savior Jesus

Christ, was someone who had witnessed the violent death of an adult child; yet she remained faithful to God and fully surrendered to His will.

"Near the cross of Jesus stood his mother" (John 19:25). As a mother, I cannot even begin to fathom such a harrowing and helpless moment. Mary's example of steadfast faith through constant prayer (Acts 1:14) and submission to God's will is a comfort and encouragement.

Faith is the first step toward grace. Faith will guide us through uncertainty and help us to surrender everything to God. Faith knows and shows that nothing is beyond God's grace and guidance. As my mother said, "No human circumstance or tragic event is ever beyond the redemptive power of God. As I expectantly abide in God's ongoing will, he can work creatively for good in every situation and help me keep on growing as I reach up to him and out to others."

After his miraculous recovery from cancer at age 30, my father replaced his question of "Why do I have cancer, God?" with "Why did I live when others die, God?" and "Why do you allow suffering?" My father's insights from his own life and death experience provide much comfort in trying to find answers.

Through the intervening years since my bout with cancer, I have forged out four immutable certainties. I now believe that these tested truths can sustain any Christian during times of crisis:

1. God is able in every trying circumstance of life.
2. God has the right to allow his children to be tested in the crucible of pain and trial.
3. God has an overriding reason for permitting us to suffer.
4. God has a reward through the suffering experience and in the aftermath of tribulation.

These four precepts have helped me catalog and put into true perspective not only my cancer experience, but also the petty, annoying day-by-day frustrations and failures that arise. I have come to the realization that I will, in all probability, be assailed frequently by unparalleled difficulties. But as his child, I can always count on him to deliver me. I have learned that whenever God puts a burden upon me, he will put his own arm underneath and sustain. Truly, "the Lord is my defense and my shield; my heart trusted in Him, and I am helped. Therefore, my heart rejoices, and with my song I will praise him" (Psalm 28:7, Berkeley).[5]

The heaviness of the plaster cast on my arm didn't even compare to the heaviness of my heart when my mother died. I didn't question my faith, but rather I questioned God:

"Why, God? Why?" I never got an audible reply or an email from Him. However, I did receive a text message from Him — or rather a message in His still voice within His text: "My grace is sufficient for you" (2 CORINTHIANS 12:9 NIV).

Embrace grace. It's a simple concept, but it can be the most difficult action to do. Embracing grace is a process of letting go, or rather surrendering to the will of God. Jesus provides the ultimate example of how to fully surrender one's will to God in the most trying of circumstances. Knowing that he would soon be put to death, Jesus prayed in the Garden of Gethsemone. "He . . . knelt down and prayed, 'Father, if you are willing, take this cup from me; yet not my will, but yours be done'" (Luke 22:41–42, NIV).

On the last day of my last visit with my mother, I experienced an incredible gift of grace. Mother insisted that she rub my feet. That was always a tradition. Whenever I was sick, she would come to my room and rub my feet to help me feel better. I insisted that she not do that this time. Her arms had brown puddles of bruises from the countless transfusions, and she was weak and had completely lost all interest in food. However, I recognized that perhaps this was her way of still being my mother and that she needed to take care of me for a moment instead of letting me take care of her. She motioned me to put my feet onto her lap. Her physical strength surprised me as she lovingly and purposely pressed and rubbed my feet to help remove my stress. A week later, she died.

Thinking about my final moments with my mother and her rubbing my feet still makes me weep. Yet, as I read and edit this section during what is now Holy Week, I am in complete awe as I just now discover my mother's actual last lesson in life to me! Whether consciously or unconsciously aware of it, my mother was uniquely following the example of Jesus and His last act of service to His disciples during the Last Supper.

"Now that I your Lord and Teacher, have washed your feet, you also should wash one another's feet. I have set you an example that you should do as I have done for you. I tell you the truth, no servant is greater than his master, nor is a messenger greater than the one who sent him. Now that you know these things, you will be blessed if you do them" (JOHN 13:14–17, NIV).

My mother's last lesson to me was to follow Jesus and to serve others. *Embrace grace.* Even though we cannot answer the question *why*, we can rest in the assurance that God's grace *is* sufficient.

Tucked inside one of my mother's boxes, I recently found a yellowed piece of paper with a poem taped on it. At the top, my mother had typed these words: "One of Margaret's favorite poems." This is her original copy that she carried with her in her favorite devotional book, *Remember Now.* The words written by this unknown author that my aunt carried with her are profound. At a young age, Aunt Margaret already realized that the question of "Why?" could never be answered on Earth, or rather "the underside." Only in heaven will we fully understand "why pain with joy entwined was woven in the fabric of life that God designed."

LIFE'S WEAVING

My life is but a weaving
Between my God and me;
I may not choose the colors,
He knows what they should be;
For he can view the pattern
Upon the upper side,
While I can see it only
On this — the under side.
Sometimes he weaveth sorrow,
Which seemeth strange to me;
But I trust his judgment
And work on faithfully;
'Tis he who fills the shuttle,
He knows just what is best,
So I shall weave in earnest
And leave with him the rest.
At last, when life is ended,
With him I shall abide;
Then I may view the pattern
Upon the upper side;
Then I shall know the reason
Why pain, with joy entwined
Was woven in the fabric
Of life that God designed.
— AUTHOR UNKNOWN

COMFORT

"Be ye angry, and sin not; let not the sun go down upon your wrath."
EPHESIANS 4:26

"Let all bitterness, and wrath, and anger . . . be put away from you."
EPHESIANS 4:31

"Cease from anger, and forsake wrath." PSALM 37:8

"And the Lord direct your hearts into the love of God." 2 THESSALONIANS 3:5

"Peace be with you all that are in Christ Jesus." 1 PETER 5:14

"And the peace of God, which passeth all understanding, shall keep your hearts and minds through Christ Jesus." PHILIPPIANS 4:7

"Peace I leave with you, my peace I give unto you: not as the world giveth, give I unto you. Let not your heart be troubled, neither let it be afraid." JOHN 14:27

COUNSEL

- Grief intrudes into our lives from many different kinds of experiences, but most often from the loss of someone or something treasured by us. Grief wears many different faces and seems to drag us unwillingly along a roller coaster ride of deep emotions. When grief presses heavily upon our hearts, we have to learn to live with it and seek to come to terms with it. There are no shortcuts to managing grief. The work of grief requires time.

  It is helpful to understand grief by analyzing the very well defined stages of grief, but those stages do not normally come in well-defined order. Grief experiences often amalgamate these tides of emotional response to tragedies in life and thus are mixed up with each other. Often those in grief find those who care deeply do not know what to say to them in grief's vestibule. Most grief-stricken folks need to know friends care, but friends do not need to feel they must interpret this grief experience.

  When a 19-year-old medical school student, the only son of a physician friend, was killed in a horrible auto accident, someone prayed, "Lord protect his family from meaningless clichés and wrong answers sometimes given by friends." A friend can often speak a special word of faith or comfort that comforts deeply. Death robs the grieving one of unfulfilled expectations, loving companionship and anticipated future blessings. Sorrow reveals the need for hope based upon faith, whether newly found or of long standing. Such faith helps one see death differently as was true of King David of ancient Israel as revealed in 2 Samuel 12:22–23. The source of comfort is ultimately the living God. Comfort may be encouraged by words that friends and ministers speak.

However, abiding comfort is found in the spiritual realities of God in one's life (2 Corinthians 1:3–5). Focusing on the tragedy of death expands the agony. Comfort and encouragement can be found by focusing on the memories of life with the deceased. A healthy prayer life is invaluable as we do the work of grief. It is not unusual for the bereaved to experience anger — toward the deceased, toward God or medical personnel. If we park with our anger and hostility it can consume us and make us bitter. Honest praying that expresses to God hostility toward Him or others, often gives opportunity for God to bring healing and recovery from grief.

The work of grieving is necessary in almost every experience of loss ... perhaps we should say in all such experiences. When denied or masked by medications or other drugs, grief cannot be dealt with in a manner that results in healthy healing spiritually and emotionally. Such masked grief will often surface unexpectedly. Perhaps the worst advice we give grievers is, "Do not cry!" Often grief needs to be experienced by shedding of tears or even deep, heaving sobs of sorrow. The Bible suggests we should not sorrow as those who have no hope, it does not say we should not sorrow (1 Thessalonians 4:13–18). There are several practical disciplines that aid us in overcoming grief and sorrow. Participating in a funeral service and accompanying the body to burial gives an emotionally healthy way to face the reality of separation death brings in this life. Returning to worship as soon as possible brings life back towards normalcy. Friends and family should be sensitive and open to times the bereaved needs to talk about the deceased in normal conversations. The mourner needs to resist withdrawal from friends or family. He or she also needs to get regular physical exercise and eat a healthy diet.

Spiritually we find great help as people of faith in God when we can consciously and specifically give up the grief and loss to God by faith and trust His loving providence to bring healing to our heartache (Psalm 147:3–4). Two little books I have found helpful: *Good Grief* by Westberg and Granger from Fortress Press; and *You and Your Grief* by Edgar Jackson, from Hawthorn Books.

Dr. Harrell Cushing (former Alabama Baptist State Convention president and director of the stewardship department [now the Cooperative Program and stewardship development office] for the Alabama Baptist State Board of Missions), was also an usher at my parents' wedding! His wife, Ann Weed Cushing, wrote the book, For Better! For Worse! Forever!.

CHRONICLING

Am I angry at God?

How have I expressed my anger?

Is my anger hurting others I love?

What else do I need to say to God?

Dear God,

Bargaining ... Bargaining

Chapter 5

Regrets, you are the smudges on the pages of my life . . .
The holes so childishly dug trying to erase mistakes . . .
The misspelled words . . .
The punctuation omitted or misplaced . . .
The big words so glibly but wrongly used before experiencing
*   their true meaning.*
How I'd like to change you, but that can never be;
For life is a rough draft essay handed in to God each day.
I can re-read, but I cannot re-write.
The lessons I learn today, though,
Can be evidenced in tomorrow's page.[1]
— CAROLYN RHEA

"This is the closest that I've ever felt to you."

After the alternative medicine stopped working for my mother, my visits to Florida became more precious and time sensitive. We would sit for hours in her small den as I wrote answers to questions in a "get to know your grandmother book." Truthfully, this was a "get to know your mother" book for me. My heart ached when she commented, "This is the closest that I've ever felt to you." Those were difficult words to hear from my own mother. This pinprick of my own regret still affects me. She didn't mean to make me feel guilty. That was my own self-inflicted wound. "You and your dad were always so close," she said. "You are so much alike. You both love international travel and meeting people. And you enjoy dreaming big like your dad." While sitting together in the den, my mother shared her heartfelt regret that she had never been able to contact the driver of the car that had killed my Aunt Margaret. She mentioned that the driver had become a pastor in Arkansas, but years ago she had forgotten his name and had no idea how to begin to contact him. She wanted to let him know that she had found peace with the will of God in her sister Margaret's life. Faith had led her to this place of peace.

During those poignant moments, I silently thanked God for bringing us closer together, and in that same breath of prayer, I asked for more time to get to know my mother even better. Unfortunately, the following week I broke my elbow. That was the bargaining stage of grief that I experienced. However, I further define "the bargaining stage" as also being comprised of guilt. Regrets bombard you like fast pitches in a batting cage. The "what ifs" are the emotional hornets that swarm and sting your conscience and leave infectious welts of inconsolable guilt. My mother writes about these incessant hornets.

Why Such Guilt, Lord?
Why didn't I . . .?
Oh, the self-recrimination, God,
Now that my beloved is dead.
Why didn't I
Make him slow down
And take time for rest?
Why didn't I

Make him lose weight
And exercise more?
Why didn't I
Insist that he not take
That short business trip abroad?
Foolishly, I thought it would help
To distance himself briefly
From the stress of his college presidency.
Why didn't I
Go with him overseas
Instead of waiting for the second trip
A few months later
As we had planned?
At times my load of guilt is too heavy to bear.
But Lord, why didn't he
Slow down and rest and live?
Why didn't he
Make time to see a doctor?
Headlong he rushed into the future
With his dreams,
Ignoring present warnings from a worn-out body.
He made these choices;
They were his own choosing.
I do not have to bear the total guilt.
We are equally to blame.[2]
— CAROLYN RHEA

Recently I discovered one of my mother's private journals. I truly felt like a thief of thoughts as I opened her red notebook to read her words written in 1984 — six years before my father's death. She wrote:

"I'm at a low today — wrestling with "weariness in well-doing" resenting the continuous bombardment of pressures upon Claude — feeling that we *have no time for getting our priorities straight — of really being together. I find myself resenting his lifestyle of going, performing, meeting another deadline, traveling — being everywhere and trying to do everything. I worry about his health — he isn't eating responsibly and there's no time for exercise." February 16, 1984*

In another box of papers I discovered a letter from my mother to my dad dated March 1951. How interesting to note the early pattern of my dad's nonstop working at such a young age in the following excerpt from that letter:

"During the meantime, before you come down Florida way, please try to slow down a little, dearest. I know that you are busy over-working yourself again. I want you feeling in top spirits when we are together, and I'm afraid you might wear yourself out before you get here. And too, I want you to take good care of your voice. You'll need it for the revival."

Grief-guilt can be more emotionally adhesive than Super Glue. It sticks to us as a reminder of what we did or didn't do, what we said or didn't say, what we wrote or didn't write. It's nearly impossible to scrub the stickiness of guilt away even with Goo Gone. Only God's grace can erase our smudges of regret and give us peace.

My mother also carried heavy grief-guilt about her own mother. My grandmother moved in with us after my grandfather died. I have a few memories of Grandma Turnage from my toddler years. She taught me nursery rhymes, and I would sit on her lap and sing. She helped build a fort in the backyard with my brothers, and she personally taught the fine skill of gardening to my brother, Claude. As I have said before, I kill silk plants. Claude and Grandma Turnage would spend hours in the yard planting flowers and pulling weeds. Grandma Turnage was fearless. I have a vivid memory of her grabbing a hoe and chopping off the head of a rattlesnake that had slithered into her garden. She was a great cook too. I still remember the taste of her bread pudding. As a child I would watch her stand at the stove and stir as the liquid thickened inside the pot. She also had the quick thinking reaction to pour hot water over my brother Randy's tongue when it got stuck to the freezer while he was licking the frost. Along the margins in her copy of *Streams in the Desert*, my mother wrote: "'Mom Turnage is a benediction in our home,' Claude used to say."

In my mother's papers, I found a treasured letter in which Grandma Turnage writes to her niece, Frances, about creating a Christian atmosphere in her home. This was written 10 years after my mother's sister died.

Chattahoochee, Florida
December 21, 1958

Dear Frances,

It was indeed a pleasure to get your nice letter telling me about your fine Christian family and your activities in the church. Congratulations! Keep up the good work. There is nothing as rewarding as living a Christian life. It is a joy to serve the Lord. Life without Christ is meaningless.

You ask me what I think was the key to Margaret's and Carolyn's Christian life. First, I would say a Christian atmosphere in the home. When we married, we established a family altar. All members of the family participated in the family altar. We always said grace before meals and each had his or her turn at saying grace. They were brought up to go to Sunday School, Church and Training Union every Sunday. Nothing other than sickness, inclement weather or a visit to Mama Ada's once a year kept them away from church. As they grew older — both taking piano lessons and Margaret voice. Carolyn was pianist on Sunday nights and Margaret singing solos and did they enjoy it! Choir practice was held each week — mostly on Friday nights (this was the junior choir) and most of the times it was held in the Turnage home. Sometimes there would be as many as 30 and their young voices would almost raise the roof of the house as they sang heartily.

Remember the Sabbath day to keep it holy! We picked the best pictures and attended in a group about once each month. Some Sunday afternoon in

Winter when the snakes had gone into winter quarters — our family and some of the neighbors' children would go on a hike into the woods in back of our pasture down to the river. There we would commune with God and nature and view His handiwork. There we saw the beautiful Torreya trees or gopher wood as they are commonly called. This section of the state (and it extends about two miles down the river) is the only place in the U.S. they grow.

Before the Baptist Church started having Vacation Bible School, the Presbyterian Church had it several years, and invited children from other churches to attend. No plans were made to go to Mama Ada's until Bible School was over at the Presbyterian Church. They went as high as they taught and won many awards — one a nice New Testament each.

Each Christmas and birthday each one received a good book — such as Elsie Dinsmore — Rebecca of Sunnybrook Farm. They built up a small library through the years. All the girls in the neighborhood that were interested in reading read their books. We subscribed to good magazines as many as we could afford. Trashy, sexy magazines were not allowed. After reading the good ones they would not be interested in the trashy ones.

They both belonged to the 4-H Club and each was president one term. They won a trip to short course twice and thoroughly enjoyed it.

Each had a small flower garden and cared for it and made flower arrangements for the home.

They learned to crochet when they were about ten years old, and through the years did some beautiful work. Coming home from college on the bus, Margaret would crochet up a breeze. When she was packing to go to Oklahoma to work with the Indians, I told her to be sure and put her crochet in that she might get lonesome and it would be something to pass the time off.

We had a pet cemetery. Everything from goldfish to dogs are buried in it. They learned early that death is inevitable and not to be feared.

Come Christmas we took off to the woods in a group to select just the right size tree and the greenery. Each passed his or her opinion on the tree and each helped decorate it. This was a family ritual observed through the years and enjoyed by all.

Margaret's passing had a deep influence on Carolyn as they had so much in common, that closeness and oneness. I never heard Margaret or Carolyn express themselves that any one particular thing influenced them to be Christians. These things in the home and school teachers, Sunday School teachers, congenial friends and many other factors influenced their lives.

Finis.

Love,

Aunt Mary

My mother's Christian walk was greatly influenced by Grandma Turnage. She underlined this passage in *Streams in the Desert*:

"My mother's habit was every day, immediately after breakfast, to withdraw for an hour to her own room, and to spend that hour in reading the Bible, in meditation and prayer. From that hour, as from a pure fountain, she drew the strength and sweetness which enabled her to fulfill all her duties, and to remain unruffled by the worries and pettinesses which are so often the trial of narrow neighborhoods. As I think of her life, and all it had to bear, I see the absolute triumph of Christian grace in the lovely ideal of a Christian lady."[3]

In quiet recognition of Grandma Turnage's lasting legacy of Christian grace, my mother wrote "Mother!" in the margin alongside this passage. Today, I, too, in quiet recognition of my mother's lasting legacy of Christian grace, wrote "Mother!"

After my grandmother's extensive cancer surgery, she was medically compromised and faced further complications. My parents realized that they were ill equipped to care for her long-term in our home. They made the very difficult decision to move her into a lovely nursing home nearby. Apparently, this decision upset my grandmother, whose generation always kept their loved ones at home and did not let strangers care for them. Mentally compromised by medication for pain, Grandma Turnage didn't understand and expressed only anger toward my mother. On Christmas Day 1966, the family visited my grandmother at the nursing home and sang Christmas carols to her. She turned her head away from us on the pillow. Grandma Turnage died the day after Christmas. Years later, my mother shared with me one of the heartaches she carried with her. My grandmother had always kept a picture of my mother and Aunt Margaret by her bedside. That Christmas, Grandma Turnage had ripped the photo in half. The portion with Aunt Margaret's photo remained by her bedside. The portion with my mother's picture remained torn on the floor of the nursing home room. That grief-guilt stuck with my mother the rest of her life, and each Christmas became a time of hidden tears for my mother even in the midst of the joy of the season. My dad always tried to comfort her with words of love and encouragement along with the fact that my grandmother was on strong pain medication that clouded her judgment and actions at that time. As one can easily note from Grandma Turnage's letter, she had always been a loving mother to my mother and Aunt Margaret. And, she was always a loving grandmother to my brothers and me.

Instead of recognizing the full scope and breadth of her mother's love across a lifetime, my mother could focus only on the final day of her mother's life and blamed herself for her own perceived failings that precipitated my grandmother's actions. In her copy of *Streams in the Desert*, my mother underlined the following passage: "If you have made a great mistake in your life, do not let it becloud all of it; but, locking the secret in your breast, compel it to yield strength and sweetness."[4] Beneath that sentence, my mother penned the secret she held within her: "I failed my mother."

Recently I learned from my oldest brother, Claude, that my mother had shared with him a deep sadness of hers during a conversation. She told him that throughout all of the years following her sister Margaret's death not once did her parents say, "Carolyn, we are so glad that you are still with us." That generational grief left an indelible mark on my mother's life. It's a reminder, too, that our words, either spoken or unspoken, have a great impact on others, even if it's unintentional. I honestly believe that my mother's parents never meant to add to her grief by this omission. They probably assumed that she would know how much they loved her and how proud they were of her. However, the reality is that children — even adult children — need the affirmation of a parent's love.

Another treasured letter I found in my mother's boxes was written by my dad's mother Chee Chee, as she liked to be called. She wrote this note to my mother after Grandma Turnage died and offered profound words of comfort.

Dear Carolyn,

This letter today is from me to you. I will write the family letter later this week.

Only wish I could be with you in person as it is hard from me to put in words what I would really like to say. It seems like I am not very good expressing myself.

One thing I can easily say is that I love you very much, dear. You always have seemed very close to me. I never think of you as a daughter-in-law, just someone VERY SPECIAL.

I know I could never take the place of a real mother. I can be second best. Just give me the chance to be understanding in all of your problems, ones that might come up now and the ones in the future.

I know you have been through some very trying times the last few weeks as well as in the past years. I think you have had your share of troubles.

You have been a wonderful daughter. What more could you have done? Please dear, don't torture yourself anymore. Mom Turnage wouldn't want you to at all.

There are times when we think we have failed our loved ones. I have felt like that many times. It is so hard to solve their problems even when you think you are doing your best.

I have come up with a solution to live by with my loved ones. I am going to do my best at all times even though it might not be. But we owe something to ourselves to.

Dear, you are going to have to do the same thing. You are such a wonderful Christian. I know you will find peace. Mom Turnage and I have had lots of good talks at different times. She always told me she was ready to go any time. Here your Chee Chee with her weak Christian faith could not bring herself to say those words like Mom Turnage. I want to live for a long time.

So with Mom Turnage's wonderful faith we can't grieve for her too much. She is where she wants to be.

So please think of your family at the present time. And not think of all the things you thought you should have done. If you don't you will get sick and then your children will suffer. You do have so much to be thankful for with your sweet family.

(Chee Chee then shares the struggles her cousin faced while caring for her invalid mother). No matter how much she tried it seems like when they get older it is one of those things. All you can do is just make them as comfortable as you can. I think those words are very true . . . I am telling you this true story of life where someone else thought they had failed until she realized she was just doing her best.

I am not telling you not to grieve for Mom Turnage. That wouldn't be right. But what I am telling you is to love your little family and be thankful for each day you have them. Some day real soon I know you will find a great peace.

And the help you have given to others in your books. They were given courage to go on in their trouble and sorrow. In your book My Heart Kneels Too page 106 'Abiding In Him', my cousin found comfort in your words. How wonderful it is you have the talent to express yourself in words to help other people. As I read your little book today there are so many passages in your book that mean a lot to me. On page 108 'Tongue Tied.' Seems to be my great trouble. I would like for you to read page 110 again. I think you will find your answer.

Love,
Chee Chee

Of course I immediately turned to page 110 in my mother's book *My Heart Kneels, Too* to see which passage would provide answers. Here is the passage:

Volcanic Soil
Sudden loss
Like molten lava
Has wiped out what I love.
Now I am desolate.
Grief has no words to pray
And yet I seek out God in prayer,
For there is hope only in Him.
In His presence
I plant my tiny mustard seed of faith
In grief's volcanic soil
And leave it in His loving care.[5]
— CAROLYN RHEA

Even though Chee Chee professed "weak Christian faith," her faith and heart in Christ were much stronger than she realized. Chee Chee had discovered the bottom line of faith: Giving it all to God. Just as my mother had written in the margin of her Bible: Forsaking All I Trust Him. In a later chapter, I will share the beautiful story of Chee Chee's passing, along with my final conversation with my dad about Chee Chee's fear of death.

I must add this side note. The day after I wrote the section about Grandma Turnage ripping apart the photograph, I discovered this entry that my mother had written in her journal about her mother:

October 28, 1992
Today is Mother's Birthday — She would be 98!!!
Thank you, Mother, for all that you did to help me <u>become</u> the person I am today — still weak but stronger. I am still in the process of <u>becoming.</u>

While mourning my father, my mother must have reflected upon the grief-guilt that she still carried about her own mother. This journal entry reflects a sense of peace and acceptance by my mother. By acknowledging the influence and impact of her mother's help through the years, she was able to move away from the final day of my grandmother's life that brought only heaviness and regret. And I love the poignancy of my mother's description of how she was still in the process of "becoming." That insight becomes even more relevant as my mother shares her experiences and feelings about finding her own identity after my father died.

For once in my life, I am grateful to be an unorganized clutter collector as I have found numerous letters from my mother that I stuffed in a variety of drawers and files. Reading these handwritten treasures is like receiving hugs from heaven. My mother wrote this message on a Mother's Day card that she sent to me in 1987:

"Dearest Meg,

It's Mother's Day 1987, an especially strategic one since my 60th birthday is only a few weeks away.

You're very close in my thoughts and prayers today. I am thanking God for sending you into my life and for entrusting me with the privilege and responsibility of being your mother. (Your father must take half of the honor, half of the credit, and half of the blame for our roles in your life!)

I simply want to tell you that I love you very dearly, that you are a wonderful person at this present moment in your life, and that I rejoice to see you growing toward becoming an even finer person!!!

Thank you, Meg, for all the joy you have brought into my life and also for the lessons you have taught me (sometimes painful ones but always meaningful ones). I ask your forgiveness for the many mistakes, both large and small, that I have made in rearing you. I pray that you will not let a single one of them cripple your life, in any way, for you have such tremendous God-given potential in every respect, (your own unique "distinctive").

I love you, Meg, dear. Consider yourself hugged!
          Mother
          (May 10, 1987)

Within that same card, my mother inserted a typed index card with the following message:

Mother's Day 1987

    To Meg, my dearly beloved daughter: Grace, mercy, and peace, from God the Father and Christ Jesus our Lord.

    I thank God . . . that without ceasing I have remembrance of thee in my prayers night and day . . .

    Wherefore I put thee in remembrance that thou stir up the gift of God, which is in thee . . .

    For God hath not given us the spirit of fear; but of power, and of love, and of a sound mind. (2 PETER 1:2,3,6,7)
          Love,
          Mother

My purpose for sharing these personal notes with you is not to boast and say, "Look at these incredible and wonderful words of love!" But rather, it is to offer a gentle reminder (myself included) to make an intentional effort to write notes of *affirmation* to our loved ones. These legacies of love will become treasured keepsakes when we are no longer here to personally share words from the heart with others. During this digital age, a handwritten letter is something that will truly last and not disappear in email cyberspace or within the text message trail. However, any mode of communication whether email, snail mail or video messaging is a blessing to those who need to hear words of encouragement and affirmation during difficult times. As I mentioned before, I still replay my mother's message on the answering machine so I can hear her voice, and I keep her letters in my desk drawer.

These tangible reminders of my mother's love have been such a blessing on the darkest of days. I am so grateful that she had handwritten love letters from my father that brought such comfort to her. (I will share the beautiful passages from those letters in a separate section.) Although I truly feel blessed to have these expressions of love from my mother, my heart weeps with those of you who perhaps never heard or read affirmations of love that you needed from your parents, children or spouse throughout your life. Please don't feel discouraged. Always remember that your Heavenly Father loves you beyond measure, and that He wrote you a love letter: The Bible. Let His loving arms wrap you close to Him so you can receive a hug from heaven right this minute!

IN MY FATHER'S ARMS

In my Father's arms, I am protected
Always loved and not rejected.
In my Father's arms, I can safely rest
Not yet ready to leave the nest.
In my Father's arms, soft words are spoken
With promises kept, never broken.
In my Father's arms, my soul is at peace.
He makes my fears and worries cease.
In my Father's arms, I find assurance
For inner strength and endurance.
In my Father's arms, comfort I can seek.
Crying with him, I don't feel weak.
In my Father's arms, no burden's too small.
He lifts each one so I won't fall.
In my Father's arms, my heart finds a voice.
With eagles' wings, I soar and rejoice.[6]
— MARGARET MCSWEENEY

The following unexpected notes of encouragement from my mother that I recently found within my piles and files of clutter have been a welcome source, especially while writing this book and working through the difficult passages to pen:

"Meg, you're quite versatile and do so many things well. I can especially admire and appreciate your gift of writing." (an anniversary card)

"Thanks for sharing your writings with me. It's always a joy to hear you read them. You're truly gifted, and I rejoice that you are using your talents so beautifully. Keep me posted!" (a random note without a date)

This particular letter remains especially meaningful. I had sent my first draft of *Go Back and Be Happy* — the true story about Julie Papievis — to my mother for her to edit. My mother had been a high school English teacher for many years in Alabama. Although this manuscript wasn't published until 2008 by Lion Hudson, my mother saw the potential and the pathway of my professional pursuit of writing. Mother was not alive when my first book, *A Mother's Heart Knows* was published in 2005 by Thomas Nelson for Mother's Day. I dedicated that book to her. I keep this very special handwritten letter inside the drawer of my writing desk:

January 9, 2002

Dearest Meg,

Thank you for sharing your manuscript with me. I marvel at your accomplishment in such a short time.

You write <u>beautifully</u>, Meg. Your prose flows smoothly and accurately. You're honoring God with this gift of writing He has given you. Your writing will be published! Your future is limitless! I'm <u>very proud</u> of you! So is your dad!

Julie is a lovely person who has come victoriously through her painful journey with God's help. By writing her story, you will enable her to be an even <u>greater blessing</u>.

I love you dearly

Mother
<u>Great job</u>!!! Keep on writing!!!

As an adult, I have an even greater appreciation and admiration for my mother. She could have chosen to live a bitter life, having lost her only sister and both parents before she turned 40 and almost losing her beloved husband at age 30. However, she chose joy and surrendered her sadness to the Lord who used tragedy to create a prayer warrior who communicated with poetic prose. Furthermore, my mother did not pass along the burdensome weight of generational grief to me. Instead, she creatively shared her love of the Lord, her love for me and her joy of writing.

My own grief-guilt is not getting to really know and fully appreciate my mother until after she died. However, the process of writing this book has been a blessing. The unexpected discoveries of my parents' love letters and my mother's candid journal entries have provided glimpses into her life and into her faith. I can readily relate to this excerpt from one of my mother's poems:

Sorting Through the Past

Books, music, programs, plans, dreams,
Diplomas, honors, awards.
Your life — reduced to paper.
But oh, what treasures they hold.
It's like putting together
The jigsaw puzzle of your life.
Your childhood,
Your high school years,
Your army years (books and letters such as those about the war crimes
*   trials in Nuremberg while you were stationed there),*

Your college years (our love letters to each other!)
Your work and ministry through the years.
I know you even better now, my love.
Father, please help me
Sort through the clutter of Claude's life and mine,
Keeping only precious treasures,
And gently leaving the rest behind.[7]

My mother's words so cogently capture my own feelings about getting to know her as I put together the jigsaw puzzle of her life by discovering clues that were left. And her line about "gently leaving the rest behind" has been such a comfort as I have struggled to "sort through the past" and the endless cardboard containers. My brother stored 122 boxes of my parents' items in his basement! During a visit to Atlanta a few years ago, I spent hours with him going through a portion of these boxes. It was physically overwhelming and emotionally exhausting to make decisions on what to keep and what to toss or give away. And the decades of accumulated dust that I encountered provoked a major sinus infection.

During that sorting process, however, I got a special hug from heaven. I was in Atlanta to officially launch Pearl Girls™ during the Christian book conference (ICRS). Pearl Girls™ is a concept based on the metaphor of the oyster. Like the oyster, women, too, encounter unexpected grit in life that gets stuck inside of our shells; however, God's nacre of love and grace covers us and turns our pain into a pearl. When women collaborate, communicate, and connect, we can make a collective difference in the world. All proceeds from Pearl Girls™ books go in full to fund a safe house in the Chicago suburbs and to build wells for schoolchildren in South Africa. The first book, *Pearl Girls: Encountering Grit Experiencing Grace* was published by Moody in 2009.

This Pearl Girls™ project became even more meaningful when I discovered a bookmark that my mother had given me years ago with my name and its meaning: Margaret means pearl! God has truly covered me with His love and grace throughout my grief, and I am so honored to encourage other women to connect and reach out to others with their personal stories, or rather, "pearl parables" as I like to call them.

In between an incessant sneezing attack in my oldest brother's basement, I opened a carton that contained a jewelry box. Inside was an antique, three-strand "pearl" necklace. This beautiful glass bead necklace belonged to my Grandma Turnage. What a blessing and an affirmation of my work to launch Pearl Girls™. Fastening this delicate necklace around my neck, I finished sorting through the endless cardboard containers with a greater purpose and focus as I wore this hug from heaven around my neck with joy.

During a quiet moment after Thanksgiving, I started reading my parents' stack of love letters. During Christmas 1949, my father wrote these words to my mother on a tiny folded card inscribed with "Christmas Greetings" on the front:

Christmas 1949

My Dearest Carolyn,

Truly a jewel is a thing of beauty, but a life that is lived to serve others and to glorify our Christ, such as yours, is my dearest, a far surpassing gem in radiance and beauty.

Pearls to me, symbolize this "Life Beautiful" that you have achieved, Carolyn. Each pearl is a result of a great hurt to the oyster's life. But the little mollusk builds an iridescent coat around this source of hurt, and as a result, the precious pearl comes into being. Life is like that too.

If we, like the pearl, can make of our hurts the basis of a thing of beauty, then we can bear witness to an on-looking world how Christians can overcome through Christ, blows that are seemingly insurmountable.

At this happiest season of the year, I give thanks to God for you, Carolyn — my Pearl of Great Price.

Your Claude

May we all realize that the guilt and grit of grief in our lives can be transformed into grace through the love of God.

Comfort

"My guilt has overwhelmed me like a burden too heavy to bear."
Psalm 38:4 (NIV)

"And ye shall know the truth, and the truth shall make you free." John 8:32

"Casting all your care upon him; for he careth for you." 1 Peter 5:7

"For he knoweth our frame; he remembereth that we are dust."
Psalm 103:14

"But there is forgiveness with thee." Psalm 130:4

"But unto you that fear my name shall the Sun of righteousness arise with healing in his wings." Malachi 4:2

"Let us set aside every weight, and the sin which doth so easily beset us, and let us run with patience the race that is set before us, looking unto Jesus the author and finisher of our faith." Hebrews 12:1–2 [paraphrase]

"And the peace that passeth all understanding, shall keep your hearts and minds through Christ Jesus." Philippians 4:7

Counsel

- When your world collapses, it doesn't usually happen in an instant. It's usually caused by a series of events. A divorce doesn't happen in one day: it often takes struggling couples years to come to the end of their ability to stay married. Post-abortion stress may take a long time to develop: when it does, it becomes a Ground Zero. Let me encourage you to turn your eyes to God and let him lead you to a place of healing. Jesus Christ has a specific design for our lives: "I have come that they may have life, and have it to the full" (John 10:10 NIV).* We don't need to relive the past. We don't need to re-experience the hurts. Pain, hurts, and disappointments don't have to keep us from a hope filled future.** *Mike MacIntosh, senior pastor of Horizon, author of "The Tender Touch of God" and "When Your World Falls Apart." *excerpt from "The Tender Touch of God." ** excerpt from "When Your World Falls Apart"*

- The bargaining/regret stage in coping with grief is what I call the "crossroad point" of the grief process. It is at this crossroad when one has a choice to remain in covenant with grief by means of regret, fault, or blame projected at oneself or at another. Or one can choose to bargain or swap their pain away with another in hopes of it leaving. The problem with regret is that it leaves a sense of guilt, which can haunt a person forever, hence making it not the best choice at the crossroad. While the bargaining stage is better than regret, this too is a form of quitting or passive surrender which will leave an "unresolved" feeling in the soul. In my personal experience, I've found that looking to something greater, such as God, is helpful. But not looking to Him to bargain, but for new beginnings. Also looking to Him not to regret, but for reconciliation. For He offers comfort, healing, and understanding, having first partaken in and overcome the stages of grief. His resolve: forgetting things which are behind and reaching forth to things before. Meaning that faith and hope are the doorway to healing, restoration, and a future, making grief a beatable adversary. *Bro. Kevin L. Tuggle, Sr., Living Word Christian Center*

CHRONICLING

What grief-guilt am I holding onto? Am I ready to give God the burden of this grief-guilt?

What would I like to say to Him?

Dear God,

Who do I need to write or call so I can affirm my love for that person?
What should I say?

Dear ___________________________,

Chapter 6

Depression ··· Depression

Are you here, Father,
In this agonizing hour of grief?
I need you so!
Surely you are near
To help me handle this.
Can it be that my eyes
Are momentarily blinded by
Tears of grief and rebellion
And cannot see that you're so very near
In this great time of need
That I stand within
The full shadow of thy presence?[1]
— CAROLYN RHEA

"Yes, Lord, I know that I'm depressed. I've no desire to live."

Those words leapt from the pages of my mother's book as I read them with shock. I had no idea that my mother was clinically depressed and did not want to live. She hid her truest feelings well from her children. Each of us lived in different states and tried to visit as often as we could. I called her on the phone almost every other day, and she would cry during those conversations. Even as an adult, I was still my mother's child, and I felt helpless that I couldn't do anything or say anything that would make her feel better. To avoid putting even greater pressure on her, I handled almost all of the wedding details on my own. However, she graciously agreed to open the response cards and keep a tally as to how many guests would be able to attend. I had hoped that my mother's opening the notes and reading the messages would be something to bless her rather than burden her. She welcomed this task and kept meticulous count. I'm not sure how long my mother's depression lasted. She died shortly after her book was released, and quite frankly I didn't want to talk about her past depression while she was battling the ever-present leukemia.

Of course, if I had fully known, I probably would have encouraged—maybe even insisted—that she seek professional treatment from a therapist for clinical depression. I actually remember asking her once during a visit if she would like to speak with a counselor about her grief, not realizing that she was actually depressed. She shook her head and said that her faith in God was getting her through the grief. Perhaps it was a generational obstacle that kept her from reaching out for professional help along with the reality that she had survived other great losses in her life solely through her strong faith in God. Bottom line, asking someone for help was always very difficult for her. My mother was the one that was always helping others.

I was completely shocked when I found this letter from one of my mother's college friends from Florida State University (FSU). I regret that I did not recognize the signs of clinical depression and that no one told me that my mother was deeply depressed. If you or your loved one is showing signs of clinical depression, I encourage you to seek professional help.

Dear Carolyn,

Thinking back to our FSU days I remember not knowing anyone as strong emotionally and spiritually as you were. I remember Margaret's funeral service and your ability to witness to all at that time and to comfort rather than being comforted. I remember your talents — writing, music, always knowing your goals and forging ahead, a talented "go-getter" who was never "pushy" and whose future seemed unlimited.

Carolyn, you say you don't know who you are and other profound things indicating your deep depression. I'm extremely concerned and feel a grief therapist is urgently needed. You owe this to yourself. I'm sure your family is concerned for you as your long-time friends but do not know what to do or say. Call your county medical society to locate a grief therapist otherwise you are going to have a long and miserable time climbing out of the pit.

You will be assisted to look within and find that wonderful person we know you are. You never lose what you've been and grown to be. This deep dark pit of misery you feel trapped in has a certain amount of self-pity associated and a feeling of helplessness. Please don't be offended by this since I speak professionally and out of love for you.

I know Claude was your best friend, lover, and father of your children but that does not make you nothing without him. Jesus is LORD. You still have Him and always will. Having Jesus enhances, not destroys. Turning your life over to Him is the greatest calling. Turning your life over to a person is not only unwise, it is destructive.

You are unique. You are precious. We expect you to be sad. You can adjust. You are a strong person and I know God has great plans for you. Remember to praise Him in all things (even in Claude's death. He could have been left a cardiac cripple instead of being taken quickly) and focus your mind on the Lord. Now! Carry on a constant dialog with Him and He will lift you up and restore you to your personal track toward greatness that maybe got sidetracked in your efforts to uplift Claude by your love for him.

Be assured that we all grieve with you over Claude's passing. Would Claude want you to go on with your life and carry on in a great and productive way? Of course he would!

Your wanting to dream about Claude is your unwillingness to let him go. Let him rest in peace and concentrate on Carolyn and her journey through life. I expect great things from you.

My mother's mantra in life was based on a verse in the Bible: "Speak the truth with love." Her friend did speak the truth with love in that letter, and I am grateful that someone professionally recognized the signs of clinical depression and gently confronted my mother with the need for treatment.

My mother's poem, "Depressed" unmasks the raw reality that even strong Christians are not immune to the darkest depths of human emotions. Yet it also reminds us that God is our Father, and He understands and lets us cry out to Him, just as His beloved Son, Jesus, cried out to Him from the Cross in human despair. Although her words are difficult to read and to emotionally process, I am glad that she shared this heartfelt anguish publicly with others.

Depressed

Yes, Lord, I know that I'm depressed.
I've no desire to live.
After all, my reason for living is gone.
I want to be with my beloved.

My body is fatigued.
Why shouldn't it be?
I cannot sleep at night.
Food repels; I am weak from losing 30 pounds.
Arthritis has flared up again,
Making it painful to walk.
Bed seems the best place to stay.

My mind is weary, too.
Tired of dealing with problems.
And of making so many decisions.
Exhausted from remembering my beloved is gone
And isn't here to cheer and help.
Sadness accompanies me wherever I go
There is no joy in living.

You say I must get up and get busy helping others?

My 93-year-old mother-in-law
Needs more of my attention?
She is hurting deeply, too?

Our daughter's wedding is drawing near,
And I must help make it a joyful occasion?

And there is a job opportunity
To teach temporarily at the college?
To use my minds and gifts?
Staying busy helping others will also help me, Lord?
Please take my hand. I want to rise and walk.[2]
— CAROLYN RHEA

Many who have lost a loved one feel stuck, not only emotionally but also physically in the land of "meanwhile." My mother had to face major decisions about where she ultimately wanted to live. My mother wanted to be with Dad in heaven and even asked God, "Why not now, Lord?" She felt that her purpose of living had evaporated into nothingness after my father's death. That proverbial black cloud of depression clouded the clarity of my mother's thoughts. Yet God, the loving Father, welcomed her questions, listened to the cries of her heart and extended His grace as demonstrated in *Why Not Now Lord?*

WHY NOT NOW, LORD?

In an instant, Lord
You translated my beloved
From earth to heaven's bliss,
Leaving me a widow,
Bereaved and hurting,
To continue life alone.
I cannot bear this pain of separation.
Why not finish breaking my heart
This very moment, Lord
And let me die, too?
We journeyed far together,
Serving You.
What joy 'twould be
To enter Heaven's gate
And meet him there!
Why not now for me too, Lord?
Your silence is your answer?
I am to stay?
Still locked in earth's mortality?
Immortality must await
God's timing?
I trust your reasons, Lord,
Though I do not understand.
Please help me.[3]
— CAROLYN RHEA

Depression was the great abyss that my mother faced. God, however, so graciously led her from that dark ledge and into His light of hope and glory, but this journey took time. I recently found one of my mother's handwritten notes to my father tucked inside her journal. In this moving letter, she shares her frustration and acknowledges her depression.

October 26, 1992

My darling,

Today is your earthly birthday — your 65th!! You would have caught up with me and would have been a SENIOR CITIZEN. You'd even be on Medicare!

But you're not. You're in God's eternal NOW, where your mortal personhood is now immortal. What joy you must be experiencing, my dear. What wonderful heavenly rewards you have earned through great FAITH and FAITHFULNESS.

I took a pot of yellow mums to your grave this morning. I sat on a little chair I had taken along and visited with you in my mind.

You'll never have to grow old and helpless. You will be eternally young and exuberant. God blessed you with an early death. How I still hope for a similar blessing.

I miss you in so many ways. I miss your phone calls opening with "You light up my life." I miss your hugs and kisses. I miss your laughter. I miss your undergirding love. I miss the music you brought into my life.

I'm lonely. I'm sad. I'm probably depressed. I have wept and wept this day. I know it's self-pity — self-centeredness. I'm leaning on the Everlasting Arms for comfort and strength. I must go on living without you.

Thank you, my darling, for loving me so dearly though all those years. Please forgive me for not showing my love for you more clearly — for not saying so more often.

The children miss you too. C3 and Meg called. I know that today has been difficult for them too — and for Randy.

I love you eternally, my darling. Never forget. How I long to see you in Heaven. I want to hear those Golden Bells.

Meanwhile, I'm trying to find why God has left me Earthbound and what He wants me to do.

Your Carolyn

Yes, I wept when my parents died, but I wept almost uncontrollably next to the casket of my brother, Randy. In a later chapter I will share why my grief was so intense at Randy's funeral. Like my father, Randy died suddenly from a massive heart attack. He was feeding a stray cat on his back deck. Randy had such a caring soul — especially for God's creatures who had lost direction in life and needed a little tenderness. He was only 53 years old.

The reality is that grief compounds grief. I don't know if there is a technical term for that emotional experience and sequence. All I know is that I have lived through it. When another traumatic event occurs in life, be prepared for more aftermath. The new grief can trigger the emotions from a prior event, either due to a delayed response (i.e., disconnected doorbell of emotions) or perhaps from the sensory memory of the other experience.

Even now, I still have my moments of unexpected tears that can occur at the most inopportune times and in the most public places — even by the produce aisle in the grocery store. The emotions of writing this book and reliving the sadness of losing my parents and brother have all been compounded by the fact that at the time of this writing, my oldest daughter, Melissa, graduated from high school and heads out of state for college in just a few short weeks. During the countdown to college, I am frantically trying to balance keeping my commitment to meet the publisher's deadline while enjoying every moment I can with Melissa. I rejoice with my oldest daughter in this great accomplishment and pray for her as she pursues the plans that God has for her. However, I also selfishly weep for myself because it's difficult to see her go. Instead of sobbing in the shower and hiding my emotions, I let my tears escape in front of Melissa and explain that I am crying because I love her and that I will miss her. Life is a process of letting go. And once again, I must let go and let grow with faith.

Tears can provide the necessary current to move our vessel of grief that is stuck in the "meanwhile" and help move it forward and onto the intended path of purpose.

WEEPING

Lord, when will my weeping stop?
The sudden shock of losing him
Shut out my tears at first,
Enabling me to handle necessary tasks
Of telling family and friends,
Making funeral arrangements,
Attending services.
Now torrents of tears flow unbidden
Each time I wake from sleep and face again
The reality of death.
And unexpected provocations trigger tears —
Seeing a caring friend,
Reading a word of comfort,
Hearing a favorite hymn,
Seeing his clothes still hanging there,
Touching an object that unlocks a memory.
I am vulnerable and cannot stem the tears.
Surely you understand, Lord,
For you wept at Lazarus' tomb.
Please enfold me in your loving arms
And weep with me.
Then, in the fullness of your time, Lord,
Let this weeping pass.[4]
— CAROLYN RHEA

And in the fullness of His time, God graciously helped my mother's weeping pass as she found her path of purpose, and He has wiped my tears too. My mother's journal entries and notes in the margins of her Bible and devotional books are tangible reminders to surrender any difficult situation to the Lord, seek His counsel, and wait for His timing. She writes in her book about grief:

I now have a deeper appreciation of the scope of the Bible: complaint and praise; guilt and forgiveness; failure and redemption; fear and courage; weakness and strength; grief and joy; suffering and healing; loss and gain; death and resurrection. I can identify with Job's anguish, Elijah's depression, and David's cries for help.

My grieving was done in the presence of God. Like Hannah of old, "I have . . . poured out my soul before the LORD . . . for out of the abundance of my complaint and grief have I spoken" (1 Samuel 1:15, 16).

My Heavenly Father, who created me and already knows all about me, listened compassionately and communicated His unfailing love and His promise of assistance — what wondrous grace![5]

I, too, now have a greater appreciation of God's Word because of my mother's notes in the margins and the way in which she personally applied verses in the Bible to help her through any difficult situation.

COMFORT

"Have mercy upon me, O LORD, for I am weak: O LORD, heal me; for my bones are vexed." PSALM 6:2

"I am troubled; I am bowed down greatly; I go mourning all the day long." PSALM 38:6

"Cast thy burden upon the LORD, and he shall sustain thee." PSALM 55:22

"And the angel of the LORD came again the second time, and touched him, and said, Arise and eat; because the journey is too great for thee." 1 KINGS 19:7

"Why art thou cast down, O my soul? And why art thou disquieted within me? hope thou in God: for I shall yet praise him, who is the health of my countenance, and my God." PSALM 42:11

"Be of good comfort, rise; He calleth thee." MARK 10:49

"He brought me up also out of a horrible pit, out of the miry clay, and set my feet upon a rock, and established my goings." PSALM 40:2

"The LORD hath heard the voice of my weeping. The LORD hath heard my supplication; the LORD will receive my prayer." PSALM 6:8–9

"When Jesus therefore saw her weeping, and the Jews also weeping which came with her, he groaned in the spirit, and was troubled, and said, Where have ye laid him? They said unto him, Lord, come and see. Jesus wept." JOHN 11:33–35

"Mine eye poureth out tears unto God." JOB 16:20

"Put thou my tears into thy bottle: are they not in thy book?" PSALM 56:8

"To everything there is a season . . . a time to weep." ECCLESIASTES 3:1, 4

"And God shall wipe away all tears from their eyes." REVELATION 7:17

COUNSEL

- The pain you're feeling is a pain that doesn't go away quickly. As a matter of fact, all the pain may never go away, but it's a reality that many, many people face every single day all across the country and across the world. Young people die whether by accident, by disease or the worst situation I think is when a young person that age takes his own life. There are a lot of other parents who have walked down this road but that in itself doesn't give a whole lot of comfort, because it's your son. There's nothing as painful in my opinion as losing a son the age of your son. If a person is 80 years old we can say they had a good life and we can let them go, but when they're 19 with all their life before them, it's so much more difficult to let them go . . . I'm saying there's no easy answer to this but I'm also saying that there is help in the process. God of course is our greatest source of help, and I would say continue to be honest with God, continue to share with God your pain and your feelings.

The other factor that helps us walk through the grief process is talking to other people about not only our pain but about our son. I would encourage you and your wife to talk about him. Don't feel like that talking about him is going to keep the pain more raw. It actually is going to help you work through the pain . . . . There's one program that's called Grief Share, and many churches all across the country have groups — I know our church does — that meet once a week . . . It's for parents who have lost children. It's for spouses who have lost spouses. It's for anybody who is going through the grief process, and the leader of those groups is trained on how to help people talk. There's something about hearing other people and entering into their world, and you realize you're not alone in the process, and you hear how others are processing it. There's something positive and helpful about that. So it would be worth searching out to see if there's a church in your area that has such a group. . . .

What we found in the study of grief over the years is that people who meet with other people and talk about their grief have a better grief experience or journey than those who don't . . . Talking to family as well as perhaps a support group or a Grief Share group is a helpful part of the process. The worst thing that you can do would be to clam up and say, "Well it's over. I'm not going to talk it about it anymore. I'm going to hold it all in and be strong here." That's the worst thing you can do. The best thing you can do is to continue to talk about the pain and continue to talk about your son and the good things you remember about him . . ."
Dr. Gary Chapman. author of the New York Times best seller, The 5 Love Languages *(These partial comments were shared by Dr. Chapman on Chris Fabry Live, September 19, 2011, Moody Radio in response to a caller who needed some guidance through grief after the death of a son).*

- When you suffer a major loss it is natural to feel a deep sense of sadness as you face the reality that you must let go of something or someone dear to you. Tearfulness, loss of appetite, difficulty sleeping, decreased socialization, and a piercing sense of loss and longing may make it difficult for you to cope as you move along your grief journey. These symptoms are also signs of clinical depression so it is sometimes difficult to distinguish a normal grief response from a major depressive disorder, particularly during the first several weeks of bereavement. As you move through the depressive stage of grieving, you may experience waves of sadness and sense of loss, often triggered by memories, holidays or special events, decisions that must be made, or conversations about the loss. You may also experience positive thoughts and memories at times as you press through your pain and try to move forward with life. While those emotional shifts may seem contradictory, they are both a normal part of the grief process. Time with friends and family is comforting as you work to take care of yourself physically, emotionally, and spiritually. Patience with yourself is key as you hold onto the hope that while the pain is deep in this stage and the sadness sometimes feels overwhelming, you know that you will eventually work through your depressive symptoms. In time you'll develop a "new normal" as you learn to adjust to your loss and move forward with life.

Depression that is part of a grief response typically subsides with time, self-care, and support. If your symptoms persist after a few months, and/or if you find that nothing brings any comfort or relief, or if you experience symptoms other than those generally identified with healthy grieving, you may be experiencing a more significant depression. Consult with a physician or a mental health professional for evaluation and treatment as soon as possible.

Nancy Williams, M.Ed, LPC, licensed professional counselor and author of Secrets to Parenting Your Adult Child.

CHRONICLING

Am I always weeping?

How have I sensed God's presence during my most difficult moments?

What would I like to share with God right now about my sadness?

Dear God,

Chapter 7

Acceptance ··· Acceptance

Peace is quiet confidence in God.
It is neither arrogant self-confidence, nor verbal boasting of
*   belief, but serene trust which meets each crisis of life.*
God — with infinite power, yet immeasurable mercy — is in
*   control of the universe; and I have placed my life in His care.*
Why should I fear my destiny?[1]
— CAROLYN RHEA

"I'm not afraid of dying. I know that I will see Jesus and be with your father again and my parents and my sister, Margaret. But I must admit that I am afraid of the physical part of death itself."

My mother and I were sitting in her retirement bungalow's living area during this difficult conversation. She was in the upholstered rocking chair, and I was sitting across from her on the sofa. Her caretaker gave us privacy and stayed busy in my mother's bedroom. I don't know what compelled me to ask that question during what would be one of my final conversations with her. At this point her appetite had waned, and she had no interest in the lobster bisque I had ordered from her favorite restaurant. She couldn't force herself to even eat a popsicle. Perhaps as a child, I needed the assurances from my mother that everything was going to be OK.

As with any difficulty in life that she faced, my mother ultimately placed her complete faith and trust in the Lord: **F**orsaking **A**ll **I** **T**rust **H**im. Her journey through grief and her own life journey both ended with "a settled peace" through God's grace. By reading her journals, I came to a deeper understanding of God's grace. Even after her death, my mother, the former high school English teacher, continued sharing lessons. The pages within this portion of her private journal became a workbook on finding grace through grief as she marked in pen a variety of definitions before refining the meaning, purpose, and application to her own life. Here is how my mother ultimately defines God's grace:

August 20, 1997

- Grace: undeserved blessings from God.
- Grace: God's unfailing love thru Christ which is expressed through His <u>divine assistance</u>.
- God's grace to me — legacy of peace.
- God's grace to others through me — a channel of God's grace.
- I shall rest in his abiding love and peace.
- Pain: Peace.

Grace is the undeserved gift of God's unfailing love and divine assistance.
1. The Gift of His Unfailing Love. His matchless love which enriches every aspect of my life. His unfailing love which cleanses my life by forgiveness of my sins through Christ my Savior who bore my sins on the Cross and continues to bless my life. John 3:16
2. The Gift of His Divine Assistance
   - in facing life's problems — wisdom, strength, courage, guidance
   - in growing more Christlike
   - in becoming a channel through which God's grace can flow out to others who touch my life.

Grow in grace—channel of God's unfailing love and divine assistance. Please help me grow in grace.

I echo those same words in my heart today: *Please help me grow in grace.* Ever the teacher, my mother left footprints of faith for me to follow. With candid vulnerability, my mother ultimately shares her own painful growth experience—a stretching process through which she discovered God's purpose for her—in *When Grief is Your Constant Companion.* But first, she needed to rediscover her "separate self" and use the gifts within her to complete God's assigned task for her life. My mother profoundly documents this painful search for herself in the following poem,

My Separate Self

Who am I, God,
Now that I'm only me?
Humbly, I stand in Thy presence
As my separate self—
Am I still Thy child,
Father, though really an adult?
Please speak to my broken heart.
You are my Beloved daughter—
Conceived in My mind,
Created in My image,
Imbued with boundless potential,
Endowed with special gifts
To equip you for your life's journey.
But, Father, I am so weak—
How can I possibly become
The wonderful person
You envision me to be?
My child, Christ will show you the way.

He is My eternal truth.
The everlasting expression of My love.
Already He is your Savior.
Let Him be your teacher and your friend.
I do trust Him, Father.
With Christ's presence guiding me,
And Thy love through Him affirming me,
Help me grow toward becoming on Earth
The person You will complete in Heaven.[2]
— CAROLYN RHEA

Identity crisis is an aftermath of grief. Everything changes, even the family dynamics. My mother expresses her increased vulnerability of being left as the only parent after my father's death. This message was typed and had never been read until I found it tucked inside a box containing my mother's papers.

October 28, 1992

Today I thought about <u>parents</u>, not individuals as Mother or as Daddy.

<u>Together</u>, <u>parents</u> form a <u>team</u>, balancing each other. When one is separate and alone after the other half is gone, the children see only the one <u>person</u>. The children now see me as I really am — without Claude's automatic balance of fun, music, laughter, dreams, joy. . . . With Claude, I too made music — with our children's songs — but now the music has ceased. Fun and laughter are silent too. I was the reality-oriented half, the "pessimist" versus the "Eternal Optimist." I am now vulnerable to the children's fresh view of <u>me</u> as I really am — lonely, withdrawn, grieving, floundering, sitting around comforting myself with junk food, etc. insecure and self-centered. Lord Jesus, please help me reconstruct my life and my relationships at this point in time.

Help me <u>love</u> my family members unconditionally.

Help me <u>affirm</u> their worth, their work, their dreams, their relationships.

Help me <u>help</u> when I should and can but not to meddle.

Help me to make wise decisions about myself so that I shall not be a burden to them.

Help me take better care of myself, physically — lose weight, etc.

Help me discover or rediscover my God-given gift or gifts and use them to honor God.

Help me reach out in Christian love to people in Bear Island or wherever I am living.

Help me learn to be <u>content</u> in the state of widowhood. I want to free Claude for enjoying his rewards in heaven.

Help me keep on growing in Thy Will.

After my parents' death, I, too, experienced a type of identity crisis. As the baby of the family, I no longer had a parent I could call to make sure I was doing the right thing as a parent. Even now I still need my parents' reassurance as I second guess my decisions and focus on my shortfalls. During a recent bout with the flu, my fever climbed above 104. As I lay on my pillow in bed, I cried out for my mother in my fevered state, recalling the cold compresses from childhood that she pressed against my forehead in the middle of the night. Even when I was a young adult living in New York, my mother would fly from Florida to take care of me after my many sinus surgeries.

As a parent without a parent who sometimes still needs a parent, I constantly turn to our heavenly Father and ask Him for guidance and wisdom throughout each stage. And of course my husband and I turn to each other. I'm sad that at such a young age, our daughters do not have grandparents. Dave's father passed away when he was a teenager, and his dear mother passed away in 2009. My heartfelt prayer is that my daughters will glean a stronger sense of my parents' lives and legacies through this book and will have a deeper understanding of my own journey through grief.

In writing this book, I, too, am gaining a stronger sense of who my parents were outside of their roles as Mom and Dad. While reading my mother's private journals, I discovered that four years before my dad died my mother had experienced a different kind of identity crisis. In this following entry, my mother expresses a deep frustration of perceiving herself as a mere extension of my dad. She mourns the loss of her own individuality.

Thursday, February 16, 1984

I feel caught up in the role of being only an extension of him and his choices. Wept and wept tonight. I love him and I have made a lifetime commitment to him but I need to find and rediscover my own personal identity along with the journey together.

Two days later in a separate journal entry, my mother composes a personal affirmation — her declaration of independence in which she proclaims her eternal love for and commitment to my dad but also claims her right to maintain her own identity and personhood through Christ. The following passages from my mother's journal provide an important lesson not only for me but also for other women who at some time in their lives might experience an identity crisis. For those of us who are spouses, parents, or guardians, we must not get lost solely in those important roles but also cultivate the gifts within ourselves.

Saturday, February 18, 1984

I feel free again to grow in my own identity even as I serve together with Claude. Tried to express this to him before he dashed off to Ocala but I don't know if he really understood or not . . .

Personal Affirmation 2/18/84

I love Claude, and I have made a lifetime commitment to him. He is the head of our household, and I have moved with him each time to his new field of service. But I cannot lock myself into total self-denial and absolute conformity to every detail of the pattern Claude has established for us in this place at this time. I shall affirm him, help him and love him; but at the same time I shall maintain the integrity of my personal identity as I keep on growing toward spiritual maturity in Jesus Christ — ultimately accountable only to God!!

What an empowering idea to have a personal affirmation! I am grateful for this legacy — a reminder that we must find and use our unique gifts to develop "integrity of personal identity through Christ." Yes, the respective personal and professional role is still important, (i.e. spouse, parent, child, teacher, banker etc.), but we must also keep intact our personal identity along the way. a separate self: A precious child of God.

In an effort to find her "separate self," my mother literally opened her front door and took the first steps to take walks outside and get to know her neighbors. She shares the beginning of that journey and her growth in grace with the following poem.

WHERE DO I BEGIN?

I'm ready to reach out to others, Lord.
But how do I begin? And where?

Find a "near edge," my daughter.

That sounds familiar, Father.
Claude and I often spoke of "near edges"
For mission opportunity, but it seems so long ago.
I had almost forgotten our favorite quote:

"Reach out and touch the near edge of a great need
And act upon it with some degree of sacrifice."*
Where are my near edges now, Father?

All around you, daughter!
Great needs are everywhere.
Begin with your neighbors.

My neighbors, Lord?
The two hundred families
In our residential development?
But we hardly know each other.
Life is impersonal here.

Get to know them one by one.
Many are hurting and need a word of comfort.
Some are lonely and need a word of cheer.
Others are sick and need a helping hand.
Some are struggling
With family problems and relationships
And need your prayers.

Then prayer is my starting point — my near edge!
I shall first reach out to them in loving prayer!
Then as I get to know them personally
Help me not to pry or judge,
But to love and affirm.
And as their needs unfold,
Help me serve my neighbor
As if I were serving Thee.
Are there other "near edges" too, Father?
Widows, Lord? Like me?
I am to help minister to new widows,
Beginning with those in my Sunday School class?
But I am weak
And not a good example for other widows.

But you understand something of their hurt.
You, too, have suffered loss.
Tell them so. Encourage them.

Then use me in Thy will and purpose, Lord.
Show me the "near edges"
Where You want me to serve.
(FROM INCLUDE ME OUT! BY COLIN MORRIS)

My mother had found and touched many "near edges" as a teacher. She often told me that education is what levels the playing field for everyone. As a young child growing up in the Birmingham, Alabama, area in the late 1960s, I witnessed one of life's most important lessons in our kitchen. Each week, Flora, a very kind African American woman, would help my mother in our home. And each week, my mother would take a full hour to sit at our kitchen table and teach her how to read and write. Before Flora passed away a year or so later, she was able to read and sign her name. She no longer had to mark her signature with an "x." My mother had empowered someone's life by simply taking the time to sit down and teach.

My mother titled one of her journals: *My Spiritual Health Record.* This notebook contained entries from March — August 1997. These entries all indicated that she was at last healing and was ready to find strength and purpose. I was especially touched by the following two entries from that journal.

5/26/97 I found this poem in Claude's papers. It speaks to me.

Every man has his Bethlehem
Source of new beginning
Where hope is born
And possibility looms large

Where history is invaded by newness
And memory gives birth to faith
Come, let us go to Bethlehem
To hear the word that comes again
Into our world
To see the light that shatters
Its long darkness
To know the God who
Meets us where we are
To feel the life that
Throbs to become
To begin again to be born
Come, let us go
To Bethlehem.
— AUTHOR UNKNOWN

5/27/97 I shall be 70 in one month! "The Lord works out everything for His own ends . . ." Prov. 16:4 " . . . Today, well lived, makes every yesterday a dream of happiness, and every tomorrow a vision of hope."

My mother found her "Bethlehem"—the source of new beginning—her ultimate growth spurt in grace by expressing and exposing with candor the raw emotions and vulnerability of her journey through grief. And in the process, she became a channel and a teacher of God's grace.

During my 20s, a friend once commented, "I would love to sit down with your mother and listen to her speak about the Lord. She seems like such a wise woman. You are so lucky." Quite honestly, I didn't read my parents' books until I was in my 30s. However, I witnessed firsthand the faith of my mother and father during my childhood and adulthood. They lived the Christian life every day. During those years, I still saw them in the primary role of parents, not "pastors." Now, I savor each printed word they left behind — in their published books and in their private writings.

Like my friend, I, too, would love to sit down with my mother and listen to her speak about the Lord. God actually answered this heartfelt prayer and provided a huge surprise: I just rediscovered the devotional video that my mother had sent to me in 1986, four years before my father died. I recall that my dad had convinced my camera-shy mother to be filmed reading from a couple of her books. After finally finding a VCR that worked in our house, I inserted the video tape. My heart raced when I saw my mother's face on the big television screen and heard her kind, lilting voice frosted with a soft Southern accent. I had forgotten how brightly she radiated her love for God. Mascara smudged my cheeks as I silently cried. Sitting on the floor, I listened to my mother speak about the Lord as she shared three poignant passages from her books. She was indeed a wise woman. Two of her stories poignantly capture the concept of acceptance. This is what my mother said:

Hello, I'm Carolyn Rhea and I'll be sharing with you today from my book HEALING IN HIS WINGS, *which I wrote as therapy following my mother's death.*

The moving van was out front loaded and ready to move again. It was time to move again. Memories surfacing. Some happy, some painful, some sad and some silly ones.

I walked through the screened back porch into the yard where the children used to play with the pets. Two dogs and a duck.

I walked past the flowers, shrubs and trees we planted that would soon belong to someone else. I even went past by our vegetable garden.

It was time to go — to leave this part of my life behind me and journey into the unknown.

Somehow I thought of Abraham from the Bible. In Hebrews 11:8 we read, "By faith Abraham, when he was called to go out into a place which he should after receive for an inheritance, obeyed; and he went out, not knowing whither he went."

And I had an imaginary conversation with Abraham:
Abraham, how did you do it?
How could you leave all that was dear and familiar
And journey bravely into the unknown?
I find it so hard to move
From one circumstance to another —
From health to sickness,
From happiness to sorrow,
From the familiar to the unknown.
God meets you there, you say?
He has gone before and prepared for you?
Make me ready, Lord, each time that I must move
From one circumstance to another.
    Strengthen my faith that You have prepared for me at my next
        destination.
Help me discard the clutter as I go along
And take only eternal treasures and necessity.
And when my last move is Earth to Heaven,
Help me face it with the calm assurance
That you have prepared the way.[3]

Perhaps you can identify with moving from one place to another, from one circumstance to another, from the dear and familiar to the unknown. You perhaps moved from the mainstream lifestyle of earning a living to the one of retirement. Have you moved from good health to chronic aches and pains or even to critical illness? Have you moved from independence to dependence and helplessness?

Life seems to be a series of moves, each one with new challenges, new pressures, new frustrations, new adjustments, readjustments, new friends, and new problems.

I remember thinking each time we'd move, "Lord how can I possibly sing the Lord's song in a strange land?" And each time in our new residence *the music came and with it the joy and the peace of knowing that Christ was there with me too and that He had already prepared the way.*

At the end of this first segment of the video devotion, my mother looks at the camera and shares words of encouragement — a paraphrase of Philippians 4:13: "And I in return could do all things through Christ who strengthens me and so can you."

I would like to say those same words to you, dear friend. You, too, can do all things through Christ who strengthens you. He has prepared the way, and he will provide the strength you need to face each move in life and to accept each circumstance.

What profound wisdom to impart — that life is a series of moves. In this video devotion, my mother gently reminded me that although nothing stays the same in life, God prepares the way for each change and provides the measure of strength we need to meet the challenges. God has so graciously guided me through my own journey of grief as an adult orphan, and He has comforted my heart as I recently moved my oldest daughter to Boston for college.

After my father died, my mother still faced several moves. She successfully battled breast cancer a few years after his death. And she at last sold the house, packed, stored more than a hundred boxes, and moved from West Palm Beach to a two-bedroom bungalow at The Florida Baptist Retirement Center in Vero Beach.

One of my mother's lessons that she shared with me was the preparation and documentation for life's final moves. When my father died, most of his important papers were not in order. Dave was extremely helpful in organizing everything. My mother resolved to get all of her own papers in order so no one would have any lingering questions as to what should or should not be done prior to and after her death. Before moving to Vero Beach, she executed a living trust in addition to a DNR (do not resuscitate) order. DNR can be an emotional and controversial topic. I fervently prayed that as one of the medical power of attorneys I would never have to confront a dreaded situation in which a doctor or EMS responder was legally bound to abide by the DNR instructions. I literally had nightmares of sobbing and pleading for Mother to be resuscitated. God knew that I was not strong enough to encounter that circumstance, and I am grateful that I didn't have to make any type of medical decision. My mother clearly and legally stated her wishes that she did not want to be artificially kept alive if her death were imminent as determined by a medical doctor. She did however insist that hydration and any type of feeding be provided if at all possible. She didn't want nourishment to be withheld even if that would prolong her natural death. I appreciate my mother's forthrightness and clear statement of her wishes. My heart aches with those of you who had to face the question marks of artificial life support with or without fully knowing of your loved ones wishes. It's hard enough to just deal with the grief.

In preparation for her final move to heaven, my mother purchased a funeral package in advance during 1998, five years before she died, and mailed each of her children a typed letter along with an information packet about the pre-purchased plot next to my father. As you can imagine, this package that arrived by priority mail one afternoon was a bit shocking at first to open and read. However, it was a gift from her heart to us and to herself. She never wanted her life or her death to be a burden to anyone. Here are some poignant excerpts from her letter.

July 4, 1998

Dearest C3, Randy, and Meg,

I'm enclosing a copy of Earl Quattlebaum's summary of my prearranged funeral plans, which we worked out together . . .

I feel that I must complete these arrangements for my own peace of mind and to make the circumstances of my death — whenever God calls me home — easier for you. We need to discuss them openly and freely before finalizing them.

The Retirement Center is to call Quattlebaum, who in turn will call Strunk Funeral Home here in Vero Beach. I do want to be buried beside your father there in Woodlawn Cemetery. I chose the same kind of casket and vault that we chose for him. . . .

I want a closed casket. Only family members can view my body. Remember that my spirit no longer dwells there. I'm in heaven with Jesus and my beloved husband and family. I shall welcome each of you someday! O glad reunion! . . .

It's so good to have such a loving relationship with each of you that I feel free to share all this with you. You know that my theme is the Bible verse: "Speak the truth in love" (Ephesians 4:15a).

I love all three of you so very dearly, and I love Carolyn, Elaine, Dave, Elizabeth, Mary, Melissa, and Katie very dearly too. Thank you for the joy you have brought into my life. I'm truly blessed.

Love,
Mother

(Handwritten on the back of my mother's letter was this note):

Please select a headstone for me and inscribe whatever you wish. Just be sure to say that I'm the wife of Claude H. Rhea Jr.

Perhaps this advanced, detailed planning was a direct result of my mother not knowing my father's final wishes as to where he wanted to be buried. She knew he had once expressed a desire to be cremated, but she made the decision to have his body flown back from Paris, instead. She needed the closure of actually seeing him one last time so she would not wonder whether he had really died or whether those were truly his remains in the urn.

My mother's second devotion in the video was also very meaningful as she provides a glimpse into her childhood Christmas traditions. This is what she said:

Hello, I'm Carolyn Rhea and I'll be sharing with you today from my book Healing in His Wings which I wrote as therapy following my mother's death that morning after Christmas a number of years ago.

Each Christmas season my father used to go down into the woods behind our home and bring us back some mistletoe. It was a present that my sister and I loved. We'd tie it with bright ribbons and would hang it over several doorways in the house.

It was always fun of course for a Christmas party, but it came to mean more than that to us. It seemed to become a symbol of the meaning of Christmas: Love. God's love for the world that prompted Him to send Christ to become our Savior. Somehow it seemed to enhance our love for each other as a family. And we found ourselves stepping under the mistletoe to give someone a hug or to plant a kiss on someone's cheek and to say, "I love you."

I thought of these mistletoe Christmases during my mother's losing battle with cancer. I penned my thoughts like this:

Illness, you ugly parasite!
Like mistletoe, you've entrenched yourself upon my body!
As you bloom and grow, you feed upon my strength.
I shall fight!
Battalions stand by to help!
My doctor's scalpel will sever you.
Modern medicine will shrivel you.
You shall fall to the ground,
And I shall stand again strong and well.
But what if I cannot conquer you?
If you are with me still
As my constant, inevitable companion,
I pray that God will help me
Learn to live with you in peace
And somehow discover how you, my enemy —
Like mistletoe at Christmas —
Can serve some useful purpose.[4]

There are times when we cannot rid our lives of things that hurt such as pain or grief, loss, illness, sorrow. Sometimes they're with us as our inevitable companions and we must learn to make peace with them.

Those are the times when we can ask God through Christ to help us transform the loneliness, the pain, the grief, the loss — symbolically into something that can serve a useful purpose in our lives. Perhaps something that could communicate messages like these:

"I'm not alone in this experience. Christ is with me."

"The grief is quite intense but I know that it will diminish with time and God's help."

"Yes the pain is there but so is the comfort of the Holy Spirit."

"Nay, in all these things we are more than conquerors through him that loved us. For I am persuaded, that neither death, nor life, nor angels, nor principalities, nor powers, nor things present, nor things to come, nor height, nor depth, nor any other creature, shall be able to separate us from the love of God, which is in Christ Jesus our Lord" (ROMANS 8:37 39).

You, too, can be conquerors!

I pressed the stop button on the VCR and took a deep breath. The last time I had heard my mother's poem about illness was at her funeral service in 2003. Feeling prompted by the Holy Spirit, I had asked my brother, Claude to somehow include this poem. His friend, Wintley Phipps, recited *Illness* with reverence and resonance and then sang *Amazing Grace*. What an incredible honor and blessing that this world-renowned man who founded US Dream Academy and who has sung for US presidents, Nelson Mandela, Mother Teresa, and even for Oprah, shared his precious time with us to read and sing at Mother's funeral.

In selecting that poem to be read, I had thought at the time that it was quite fitting and symbolic of my mother's battle with leukemia. Just as she had made peace with her "inevitable companion" of grief after my father's death, she accepted her "inevitable companion" of a terminal illness. And when my mother's last move was Earth to heaven, God helped her face death with the calm assurance that He had prepared the way.

After watching her devotional video, I now understand the poignancy of the mistletoe story and how it relates to Grandma Turnage. I think the mistletoe was my mother's own parasitic guilt about having to move her mother into a nursing home. Through Christ's strength, my mother became a conqueror of this heavy burden by transforming the guilt into a reminder of grace: Love. As my mother said on the video, mistletoe became the special memories of family love expressed with joy and laughter during the Christmas season. However, she adapted a practical application and goal for herself because of this emotional experience. One of the reasons my mother chose to move to the Florida Baptist Retirement Center in Vero Beach was that this community offered a step-up facility to accommodate changes in health. The two-bedroom villa that she rented there for over five years was part of the independent living area. An assisted living and even a nursing home facility were also located on the same campus. Mother told me that she never wanted to be a burden to her children and to our respective families. During my 30s, she once said, "I want you to know that I'm in my right mind, and I give you my full permission and blessing to put me in a nursing home at any time you and your brothers feel it is appropriate. I do not want to live in the homes of my children." She was adamant about this wish. With fresh hindsight, I more fully understand that she was still harboring some guilt about placing her own mother in a nursing home and wanted to shield her children from any future regrets.

Writing this book has given me the precious opportunity to remove my own tangled "mistletoe" from the tree of self-pity and to symbolically hang it instead in my home as a reminder of the lasting love of family and the eternal promise of God's love. This process has been a time of revealing and healing.

Nearly a decade after my mother's death and more than 20 years after my father's death, I at last have a settled peace within my heart. Although I continue to miss my parents, my brother Randy and my grandparents during the "meanwhile," I know that because of my faith in Christ, one day I will spend eternity with these loved ones who have passed on. I look forward to meeting my Aunt Margaret and thanking my parents in person (or rather in spirit) for all that they did to foster my faith and my love for God.

I thought it would be quite fitting to end this chapter with the last letter that I found in my mother's papers. For some reason, she never mailed this to any of us but instead left it with her prayer journals to one day be discovered and read. I would like to share her final words of wisdom with you, dear reader.

Friday, June 16, 2000

My dearly beloved family,

I feel especially close to you today and to my beloved husband — your father.

I'm counting my blessings. God has blessed me far beyond anything I deserve — grace gifts!

What a wonderful 70th birthday celebration you gave me! We were all together again! What treasured memories I have of that experience. Thank you with all my heart.

I shall be 73 in a few days. I'm still 72 today, Mother's age when she died. I have no desire for longevity. I'm ready whenever God calls me home.

Remember to "speak the truth in love" and walk life's journey with faith and courage. Jesus is with you.

I love you.
Mother/Mimi/Grandmommy

Comfort

"The Lord is my strength and my shield; my heart trusted in him, and I am helped: therefore my heart greatly rejoiceth; and with my song will I praise him." PSALM 28:7

"I have fought a good fight; I have finished my course; I have kept the faith:" 2 TIMOTHY 4:7

"Neglect not the gift that is in thee," I TIMOTHY 4:14

"But by the grace of God, I am what I am:" I CORINTHIANS 15:10

"For we are his workmanship, created in Christ Jesus unto good works, which God hath before ordained that we should walk in them." EPHESIANS 2:10

"May the God of peace....equip you with everything good for doing his will, and may he work in us what is pleasing to him, through Jesus Christ, to whom be glory for ever and ever. Amen." HEBREWS 13:20 21 (NIV)

"let us run with patience the race that is set before us, looking unto Jesus the author and finisher of our faith" HEBREWS 12:1 2

"Ye shall go out with joy and be led forth with peace:" ISAIAH 55:12

Counsel

- We have a basic choice to shape our lives according to reality, or to try to shape reality according to our lives. Sometimes reality can be changed. We would lack most breakthroughs in science, in the arts, and in physical performance were this not so. But sometimes reality is unbending, despite our deepest desires and strongest efforts.

When my mother was dying and no manner of medical intervention, no pleas to God for miracles seemed to be changing her condition, our acceptance of reality helped her to die well, and helped us to properly grieve. It helped her to die well because once we accepted that death was not only inevitable but near, we no longer sought medical treatment that would prolong her life (and her suffering). There is a natural shutting-down process that the body undergoes, and when we brought my mother to her home and away from the drugs, feeding tube, and hydration that were of no benefit to her, she died relatively quickly and painlessly.

And our acceptance of reality helped us to grieve by shifting the focus of our hope from miraculous cure to deliverance from suffering. Without knowing it, we were already anticipating life without my mother. When she did die, there was genuine sadness, but no shock, not even surprise. We knew it was coming.

I've found another layer to acceptance—that of accepting grief itself as part of my reality. Just like there is a natural shutting down to human life, there are manifestations of grief that are, if not standard, certainly not unusual. I accepted things like fatigue, rawness of emotion, loss of focus, and introspection as part of my grieving for my mother. And though it has been more than two years since she died, there was a time not long ago when I impulsively thought, "I have to call Mom and tell her about that," only to realize a moment later that I couldn't do that. And to accept once again that the world is not the same without her in it, nor am I. Pastor Don Wink, senior pastor, Lutheran Church of the Atonement Barrington, Illinois)

- Grief is universal. The facial expressions, the feeling, and the types of people we grieve. The expression, however, is as different as the people are. When a person experiences this universal process, it may or may not be about death itself but about the loss. It is a cry that "someone or something was important to me, held meaning for me, and I feel the emptiness where that person (or thing) once was." Grief cannot remain sad, however. It must complete itself through the amazing human phenomenon of filling the emptiness. This is done in many ways, healthy and not, but a healthy grieving process includes accepting the reality of the loss, mourning appropriately and adequately, and finding positive meaning to place in the emptiness where the void is. This is called "healing." We begin this life as egocentric and spend it learning what is more important than the self. The unique opportunity afforded us by grief is that we are able to be completely selfless when we feel completely selfish. Serving others is a precious opportunity during the grieving process. It is a death to self. This is called "faith." This death is only logical by the foundations of serving a God who loves people selflessly. Those who wish to belong to God may walk in the footsteps of Jesus. He served unto death, and therefore, during our darkest hour, we may serve even then because there is a sparkling light at the end of that long tunnel: ever-deepening intimacy with God through the Resurrection. This is called hope. Once hope is found, joy is not far behind.

Austin Ward, M.S. Counselor Health Connect America

CHRONICLING

How has my identity been altered through this grief?

What are the "near edges" in my community or in my church?

What gifts and strengths do I have that can help "touch a near edge of a great need"?

Chapter 8

A Comfort Box

When something I love is taken from me — whether merely
a toy or something of far greater value — just as a
child, I cannot understand, and I cry loudly in protest.
Then it is that my Father calls me to Him that He might wipe
my tear-stained face.
Gently He lifts me, rocking me in His strong arms.
Quietly He soothes my sobs and softly assures me that
together we can make the loss a gain.
His spirit calms my own, and I view my sorrow with the
serenity of new perspective. My Father has promised to
help!
Tired and spent, yet filled with peace,
I rest in the security of His love and understanding.
Such is comfort.[1]
— CAROLYN RHEA

"C3 sent me his beautiful tribute to your father called 'Dark Chariots of Bright Grace' — that was one of your dad's favorite quotes. C3 has your dad's gift for eloquent prose."

My mother had called to share this news with me. She was deeply touched by what C3 had written and sent a copy of it to me. This favorite quote of my dad was borrowed from a passage written by C. H. Spurgeon and featured in the devotional book, *Streams in the Desert:*

"How can we have rain without the clouds? Our troubles have always brought us blessings, and they always will. They are the dark chariots of bright grace. These clouds will empty themselves before long, and every tender herb will be gladder for the shower. Our God may drench us with grief, but He will refresh us with mercy."[2]

After my dad's death, Mother kept what she called her comfort box—nothing fancy; merely a small blue, plastic storage container with a latch-box lid. Although she had told me about it, I had never seen the actual comfort box until I opened one of the many moving boxes stacked in my closet. Inside this comfort box, I found letters and sympathy cards that family, friends, former classmates, and others had mailed, in addition to a few fan letters she had received from those who had been touched by her books. Inside her comfort box, I found the copy of that beautiful essay written by my brother, Claude Rhea III aka C3.

Dark Chariots of Bright Grace

A fierce storm lashed West Palm Beach through the pre-dawn hours of Wednesday, September 19, 1990. The imposing ficus tree standing aside the president's office at Palm Beach Atlantic College barely quavered in the gusts and torrents.

Two years earlier, my father had rescued it from a construction area, with some assistance from a five-story crane. The ficus flourished in its new location, providing pleasant evergreen canopy to that corner of the campus. It was Dad's favorite tree.

Lightning splintered its frame in an instant.

That afternoon, Kathryn Grant accompanied my mother to survey the fallen ficus. While they pondered the scene, another life was felled across the Atlantic.

An unsmiling agent was awaiting my arrival at the ticket counter of the Little Rock airport. He handed me a hastily scribbled message that read, "Call your mother — Emergency."

Within moments, she imparted those dread words that I had relegated to some distant future date. "Son, your father has died."

As the aircraft ascended above verdant Arkansas rice fields, the finality of those words numbed and pierced my soul. The hymn writer had prophetically described my grief; "when sorrows like sea billows roll." Waves of unfathomable sorrow upwelled and broke against my heart. How could it be "well with my soul?"

An expanding circle of loving friends, though separated by miles, began upholding my family in prayer. God answered their prayers by providing tangible reminders of His presence and His love.

As the flight descended into Memphis, a rainbow graced the pallid eastern sky. It arched heavenward from the placid waters of the Mississippi. Yes, the hymn writer also spoke of "peace like a river attending my way."

Resplendent rainbows had punctuated my preceding weeks with serendipity. From the Grand Canyon's depths, twin arcs of color had radiantly embraced the sky. Just that Sunday, another had brightened my journey along Interstate 66 toward the refreshing koinonia of Columbia Baptist Church.

God's faithfulness spans life's spectrum!

Mother and Dad had shared the delight of watching their two "lovebirds." The feathered couple perched on the housetop for days. Nothing could separate them.

After Dad departed for Paris, Mother returned home to the presence of a lone mourning dove. She glanced about for its missing mate with strange anxiety.

I wept as I wondered how to tell our three-year-old daughter, Elizabeth, about Dad's death. She had relished the special times with her beloved Granddaddy, particularly flying her Big Bird kite over the dunes of Riviera Beach, Florida.

Elizabeth's mother and I led our daughter to the side yard where I gently told her, with a faltering voice, "Granddaddy is with Jesus." A dove reposed on the garden gate just behind her. Quietly, it observed our conversation.

Mother arose early the next morning. Outside of the kitchen window, Dad had cleared a small plot intending to create a magnificent flowerbed for her. She watched "her dove" alight in the clearing. Two adolescents scampered out of a nearby clump of jasmine bushes to greet her. The three affectionately preened and caressed one another.

God's bright grace lighted upon us as kindred doves. With renewed appreciation, we celebrate the blessing of family.

During his youth, Dad considered becoming a doctor. He chose to pursue ministry through music and education. God healed him from cancer, and he sang and testified tirelessly of the Great Physician, our Balm in Gilead.

Many friends visited Mother to express condolences. One individual added his abiding gratitude. A few weeks earlier, Frank Wright had met Dad and Judge Paul Williams for lunch in Palm Beach. During their meal, Frank suddenly stood, unable to breathe and turning blue. Dad rushed behind him and executed three Heimlich maneuvers, dislodging the obstruction. He saved Frank's life.

Mother and I stood silently beside Dad's open casket. His life partner of 39 years then spoke with calm assurance through her tears, "I know he's not really here. This is only his earthly shell. He is alive in the presence of the Lord he loves."

I read to our encircled family the Bible's assuring admonition, " . . . be ye steadfast, unmovable, always abounding in the work of the Lord, forasmuch as ye know that your labor is not in vain in the Lord." We thanked God for Dad's life, for his labors and for his legacy of love.

As a solitary bagpipe effused the endearing strains of *Amazing Grace* during Dad's memorial service, I smiled. That morning a precious new sister in Christ, stirred by the College family's remembrance and celebration of Dad's life, had accepted Jesus as her Savior in a professor's office.

Jesus Christ fills even death's dark chariot with bright grace!

Dad's last words were, "I think the Lord wants me home. I don't understand it because I have so much to do. Tell Carolyn that I love her."

Three physicians vainly labored in the emergency clinic of Charles deGaulle Airport to resuscitate his failing heart.

God's bright grace dispelled death's darkness as Dad entered — certainly with singing — into the glorious presence of his Blessed Redeemer![3]

After my mother's death, I started my own comfort box, or rather a comfort drawer at my writing desk. There, I stashed letters to me from my parents and Chee Chee. Whenever I need a quick energy boost and words of encouragement, I pull open my desk drawer and savor their words. I will also include this beautiful essay written by my brother in my Comfort Box.

Already in my Comfort Box is my mother's Easter card to me from 2001:

Easter has more personal meaning for me since your Dad's death. Because of Christ's resurrection, your Dad now lives in another dimension, and we shall be together again!

I love your writings, Meg. They touched my heart. How great to see you growing spiritually. I've read them over and over again. I believe that God is going to open the door for publication. Keep on writing!

I think the concept of having a separate place to store tangible, treasured memories is a great idea. If I were more organized and had more time, I would love to decorate an actual comfort box and accompanying scrapbook a la Creative Memories™ style. However, even my Valentine's Day boxes from childhood left a lot to be desired from the decorating perspective. The beauty, however, is found within the comfort box.

The following letter from my mother is a new addition to my comfort box. I found it amongst my mother's papers. For some reason, she never mailed it to all of us.

Father's Day 1993

Dear C3, Randy, and Meg,

I know that you will be missing your father in a special way this Father's Day. I know that you have been hurting all along, but I have been so caught up in my own grief that I haven't mentioned yours often enough. Please forgive me. I want to use this opportunity to share some things with you.

I hope the "music" stationery will call to your remembrance your father's special God-given gift of music, which he used to God's honor and glory.

Inside the card you will find a copy of the words to "Lord, Make Me an Instrument of Thy Peace," a song that your father loved. It is a Xeroxed copy of John Templeton's Thanksgiving 1990 card to us. That has special meaning now that Chuck Colson has won the Templeton Award for his ministry at Prison Fellowship. I admire him for giving all of the award money to Prison Fellowship. C3, you were instrumental in getting things underway to make it possible. I'm proud of you for following God's prompting to do so. Your father used to say that it didn't matter who got the credit. What mattered was that you quietly did your part. Meg, I'm glad that you went to the reception for Chuck Colson in New York and that you were able to speak to John Templeton. Randy, John Templeton was the first recipient of the Free Enterprise medal that your father started at Palm Beach Atlantic College. John Templeton is world renowned in the area of investment. He is a wonderful Christian.

I'm also sending you a Xeroxed copy of a letter from Tim Owings. Randy, Tim was pastor of First Baptist Church there in Tuscaloosa. I think you met him. I don't know if you, C3, and you, Meg, have met him or not, but you might some day. He is now pastor of First Baptist Church, Augusta, Georgia. I treasure his letter and keep it in my Comfort Box.

I also keep Estelle Slater's letter in my Comfort Box. Estelle is from Carollton. She served as an Associate in the Southside Baptist Student Union Department.

In closing, I want to share this quote with you, for it is so true of your father. It is by Beecher and is found on page 164 in one of my favorite books, Streams in the Desert. It is my mother's copy of the book, and I treasure it.

"When the sun goes below the horizon, he is not set; the heavens glow for a full hour after his departure. And when a great and good man sets, the sky of this world is luminous long after he is out of sight. Such a man cannot die out of this world. When he goes he leaves behind him much of himself. Being dead, he speaks."[4]

I pray that your many happy memories of your father will blanket your life with love and will bless your Father's Day.

I am so blessed to have you three wonderful adult-children. I am proud of each one of you. Your father is proud of you, too.

And this I pray, that your love may abound yet more and more in knowledge and in all judgment; That ye may approve things that are excellent; that ye may be sincere and without offence till the day of Christ; Being filled with the fruits of righteousness, which are by Jesus Christ, unto the glory and praise of God. Philippians 1:9–11

I love you very dearly.

P.S. I decided to include something else — four pages from my writing, which have been my therapy. I call my "book" The Wilderness of Grief. Its subtitle is A Widow's Wanderings in the Wilderness of Grief. It is dedicated to "My Beloved Husband, who awaits my coming."

I'm enclosing the first page, "Acquainted with Grief," the scripture references for that page, "Thy Will, Thy Way, Thy Time," and the scriptures for that page too. I am truly learning to pray "Thy will, Thy way, Thy time" about many things in life.

I never received this letter while my mother was alive; yet each time I read it, my heart overflows, not only with tears but with the comfort she conveys in this typed letter. After reading this Father's Day letter, I was quite curious to find the specific letters my mother references that she keeps in her comfort box. I was curious to read the words in these letters that ministered to her grief in hopes of revealing comforting messages that could be shared with others who grieve. Sorting through the large stack of letters, I at last found the two referenced. Here are some meaningful excerpts:

January 1, 1991

Dear Carolyn,

You and Cecile (Chee Chee) and C3, Randy and Meg have been so very much in my prayerful thoughts. How difficult it is to put on paper my deep feelings of love and sympathy.

For half a century Claude has been one of my most favorite people. I've always thought of him as a "little brother."

The summer of '49 was special when Claude was chosen as a student missionary to Hawaii — returning with the exciting news that he had found the girl of his dreams.

Shortly afterwards as a brand new member of the BSSB's Student Department, my very first field assignment was a tour of Florida campuses. O joy! Now I would get to meet in person Claude's Carolyn. And indeed I did. As I walked into FSU's BSU Center, my first words were something like: "Where's this Carolyn Turnage? She'd better be the greatest to measure up to 'my' Claude!" A chorus of voices responded: "That Claude Rhea had better be near-perfect for our Carolyn!"

Do you remember how at that retreat, you and I sneaked away every opportunity we had to huddle and talk about "who else"?

How very right you two have been for each other.

Carolyn, your writings have meant much to me and to many others. I still read your little volumes over and over. I have given especially Such is My Confidence as gifts countless times. O, that it were still available . . .

What beautiful meaningful memories we have of Claude whose committed life and dedicated talents were used by God in such a marvelous variety of ways.

My prayers continue for you and yours.

I love you,
Estelle Slater

Estelle's letter was beautifully written and shared special memories about my parents' courtship and marriage. I think that is an important element to include in writing a sympathy card to someone who has lost a loved one. Include personal anecdotes and fond memories within the note. Writing the name of the loved one is important too. I often find myself purposely avoiding writing the name in sympathy cards and instead inserting the words — your beloved husband or your beloved wife — thinking that by writing the name it would intensify one's grief. Now I will intentionally include the loved one's name and recognize in writing the legacy that person leaves by sharing a fond memory if at all possible. In addition, the letter that Estelle wrote recognizes my mother's unique accomplishments separate from that of my father's. I think that was especially meaningful to my mother as she carefully cultivated her "separate self" by writing books.

The additional letter referenced by my mother was written by Tim Owings. Here are his words of comfort:

October 9, 1990

Dear Carolyn,

I have waited these many days to write because I could not find the words to express my grief over the death of Claude. Kathie and I have wept every time we read an article about his passing. Both of us feel a deep personal loss and emptiness knowing we will have to wait for heaven's reunion.

Our pain cannot be compared to what you and your family must be experiencing now. The days have grown to nearly three weeks. No, I can only imagine how loud must be the silence in a place Claude called "home." I want to hear him sing again "if with all your hearts you truly seek Him" and a hundred other songs made holy by his voice. How heaven must be enriched by his song added to the host of saints now praising our Lord Christ.

Perhaps a story about my relationship with your beloved Claude might help both me and you take another step toward healing our grief. Nineteen years ago, I was a freshman at Samford, majoring in music (piano and voice). One day, in fact, one morning after a frustrating piano lesson, I walked into Claude's office — no appointment — hoping he would have a few minutes to see me.

He did — he always did — we talked. Well, I talked a few minutes and he listened with loving patience. I don't remember what he said, but I will never forget what I heard. I heard God affirming my 18-year-old, homesick, not-so-sure-as-I-thought-I-was life. He took my very being and in a few minutes, did open heart surgery.

I never got over that. I walked out of his office on a new path, with a new hope and a new friend. When you've been loved like that, you never forget.

Of course, I'm not relating something you did not know. You knew Claude as no other human being could know him. You knew him to be just like that. So, as I type this letter with tears wetting my hands, I can only weep for you my sister, my friend, the one person this side of heaven who is my link to Claude. I pray for you and yours. Many sorrow with you.

Carolyn, Kathie joins me in thanking you and your precious children for sharing Claude with us and so many thousands of God's children around the world. With unselfish extravagance, you let him be the free person under Christ he was created to be. You gave him your love and your blessing. For that, all of us who were loved by Claude are forever grateful.

I would write more, but I can't go on right now. Know that you are in our prayers daily. What God began through his life is now loose in us all. With God's help, Kathie and I will be stewards of the gifts Claude gave us. You are loved.

As always,

Tim

This beautiful letter also often mentions my dad by name and reaffirms my mother's deep feelings of grief. In addition, Tim shares special memories and personal reflections about my dad. I found it quite interesting that my mother actually made marks on this letter. She put wide brackets around the section in which he and his wife thank her for sharing Claude with unselfish extravagance. Someone's recognition of my mother's personal sacrifice through the years helped comfort her.

There is a postscript to the story of this letter. Prompted by God, I "googled" Tim Owings and found a contact number for him. I picked up the phone and called him to share how his letter had touched my mother's heart and that she had saved this note in her comfort box. I also asked him to prayerfully consider writing some words of wisdom for the Counsel section, and he graciously accepted. I think it is fitting that Tim's words of comfort be included in this chapter.

A comfort box is an excellent way to deal immediately with the overwhelming intensity of grief. For those who are grieving, consider making a comfort box by gathering meaningful photographs, keepsakes, and cards and then, place them into an easily accessible container or drawer. Also, write down Bible verses or quotes that are helpful, in addition to books you would like to read at some point. For those who are the comforters, perhaps you can help create or decorate a comfort box for the one who is grieving. After my brother Randy's death, a sweet friend, Cathy Eidson Brown, sent a lovely comfort basket. This wired basket was covered in ribbons with tiny pink and green scrolls attached. The pink scrolls have typed prayers and verses from the Bible in which she inserted my name: "Father, may Meg know your strength and courage; may she not be frightened or dismayed, for You are her Lord God and with her wherever she goes" (Joshua 1:9). The green ones have typed words from songs or hymns. I treasure this blessing from Cathy. Reading these personalized promises from God provides true comfort.

Yes, our ultimate comfort comes from the Lord; however,

keeping a comfort box around for those sleepless nights and moments of weeping provides a tangible means in which "many happy memories will blanket your life with love and will bless."

In her letter, my mother mentioned that she was learning to pray "Thy Will, Thy Way, Thy Time" about many things in life. She writes:

THY WILL, THY WAY, THY TIME

Thy will?
Father, was death at 62
A part of Your perfect will for Claude's life?
Did You plan everything from the beginning?
Had he completed Your purpose
For his earthly life?
Having finished his work,
Did he die in Your way and time?
I wonder.
Thy way?
Father, did You intentionally create
The circumstances in which he died?
Or did You work lovingly and creatively
For his highest good
Within circumstances
Brought about by life choices —
His and others?
My heart ponders.
Thy time?
Father, was it really Your scheduled time
For him to die?
You could have intervened
And spared him yet again, but You didn't.
Father, as my frail mind contemplates

Your omnipotence,
I kneel in reverent awe.
My human understanding of Your divine will
Is meager indeed, yet I am confident
That unseen aspects of Your wise and loving will
Prevailed in Claude's death.
I can safely trust You with the unknown.
Claude loved You and trusted You.
So do I.
Thy will. Thy way. Thy time.
In my life, too, and in my death.[5]
— CAROLYN RHEA

COMFORT

"The LORD gave and the LORD hath taken away; blessed be the name of the LORD." JOB 1:21

"And he . . . kneeled down, and prayed, saying, Father, if thou be willing, remove this cup from me: nevertheless, not my will, but thine, be done." LUKE 22:41 42

"For my thoughts are not your thoughts, neither are your ways my ways, saith the LORD. For as the heavens are higher than the earth, so are my ways higher than your ways, and my thoughts than your thoughts." ISAIAH 55:8 9

"I will meditate in thy precepts, and have respect unto thy ways." PSALM 119:15

"All the days ordained for me were written in your book before one of them came to be." PSALM 139:16 (NIV)

"To everything there is a season, and a time to every purpose under the heaven." ECCLESIASTES 3:1

"My times are in thy hand." PSALM 31:15

COUNSEL

- Grief is a journey, a verb, a movement, a transition not of our choosing. Like opening our eyes into a moonless, lonely night, darker because the stars seem blotted out by tears, grief suddenly, brutally shows up. If we stay on grief's journey, with the passing of time and the good and nourishing grace of God, we come at last to the place of acceptance; a place punctuated both by terror and promise. Terror, because we realize that to accept our loss is to finally admit to ourselves there is no going back to wherever "there" may have been. Promise, because in the generous, wide place of acceptance, loss may be transposed into hope, sorrow into gratitude, self-pity into resurrection. This transforming power of acceptance is so often overlooked, even unnamed. We fearfully think that acceptance of loss diminishes our memories when actually the opposite is true. Acceptance places us in a new and renewing reality where life can blossom again and again. Far from being a final "phase" of grief's journey, acceptance is actually the place of new beginnings where dawn's light breaks the horizon of sorrow's night; where for the first time in a long time, we remember that God is the author of the new. It bears noting that our Lord Jesus Christ rose into resurrection life on the first day of the week. Such is that day for us that can become the rest of our story, lived in God's new place made possible embracing and being embraced by acceptance. Yes, grief is a long journey into a night not of our choosing. But the gift of God is life eternal, a gift we simply and at times tearfully accept with deep gratitude.

Timothy L. Owings — former pastor and author of an important letter in my mother's comfort box

CHRONICLING

What items would I put inside a comfort box?

What are my happiest memories and recollections of my loved one?

How did this special person in my life impact or change me?

Chapter 9

Handles for Helping

My dear,
What if death were reversed
And I had died first?
You would have grieved, yes;
But you would have continued
With your work of helping others —
Young people through Christian education,
And multitudes through your gift of music.
Your handles for service
Would still be in place
You'd simply continue as before,
Though probably at greater pace.
I have no ready handles now, Lord?
Please show me fresh new ways
That I can help others
And thus serve Thee.[1]
— CAROLYN RHEA

"You honestly think I should pursue getting my book on grief published?"

As an accomplished author, my mother's hesitation to seek publication for her manuscript surprised me. How could she have any self doubt? My mother, Carolyn Rhea, was one of the first Christian authors of the twentieth century to have original material (not previously published) to be acquired by Grosset & Dunlap, a major New York publishing house (now part of the Penguin Group). Two of my mother's devotional books were featured in what was then the newly established "Famous Books for Spiritual Guidance and Inspiration: The Family Inspirational Library." On the back cover, my mother's name and her two books are listed alongside the names of several giant Christian authors throughout the centuries and their respective works acquired by Grosset & Dunlap for The Family Inspirational Library. A sampling of names include: Charles H. Spurgeon (*Daily Food for Christians*); Thomas a Kempis (fifteenth century author of *The Imitation of Christ*); Andrew Murray (*Abide in Christ*); Charles Sheldon (*In His Steps*) and the list goes on. She then went on to write books for Broadman Press (now B&H) and Zondervan. How could she be fearful of pursuing a publisher for her grief book?

Grief is intangible and intense. Therefore, it is important to find tangible "handles" to hold onto during this emotional journey. My mother found her handles for grief first by clinging tightly onto her lifeboat of faith and crying out to God throughout the intensity of the thunderous and incessant waves. But during the calm of the storm, my mother discovered that God still had plans for her and for her compilation of writings, a dissertation of grief she had penned — sometimes during many sleepless nights. In her personal journal, she writes:

Sat. March 8, 1997 — This time last year I was still taking radiation. One year ago last night, I dreamed that Claude came back — bright and radiant — hugged me and affirmed our love. His work on Earth was finished. Mine isn't.

. . . establish the work of our hands . . . . Psalm 90:17. Please help me finish Outpourings and dare to fail or to succeed . . . .

Six years after my dad's death, my mother was diagnosed with breast cancer and underwent surgery and radiation therapy. However, she continued to pour out her heart to God with her writings and paired corresponding Scripture verses next to the poetic prose. As previously mentioned, my mother was not completely certain that the Lord wanted her to pursue publication. I found this notation she wrote on the bottom of page 306 in her copy of *My Utmost for His Highest*:

"Father, if your purpose is to use my book to help comfort other widows, give me the courage to pursue its publication and to be vulnerable to criticism."

I actually now understand her hesitation. It's difficult to put one's vulnerability into print and open one's heart and words to criticism. However, I am glad that she followed God's prompting to pursue publication and that New Hope Publishers published what would be my mother's final book at age 75. In the end, my mother's book about grief comforted me while I grieved for her. And ultimately, her courage to express vulnerability encouraged me to share my own journey of grief with you, dear reader.

My mother underlined the following passage in the August 6 reading of the devotional book *Streams in the Desert*. Somehow that must have been the encouragement she needed to hear to pursue publication. Next to this passage, my mother wrote: My prayer for Outpourings (the working title she gave to her book) 2001:

"Child of Mine, with comfort wherewith thou art comforted, from this time forth, go comfort others, And thou shalt know blest fellowship with Me, Whose broken heart of love hath healed the world."[2]

Writing had somehow always been her helping handles through grief. She wrote her first book, *Such Is My Confidence* as a means of healing years after her sister, Margaret's death. And my mother wrote *Healing in His Wings* as therapy following her mother's death. Her final book *When Grief Is Your Constant Companion: God's Grace for a Woman's Heartache* was my mother's therapeutic and interactive workbook with God during her wandering journey through widowhood. She candidly struggled with her feelings of sorrow in context with God's will and His remaining plans for her. Writing transformed the intangible into printed words. By putting her thoughts, feelings, and grievances onto paper, she was able to then confront facts and complete a cardio-intense workout of her faith in the Lord.

Writing to work through grief apparently runs in the family. After opening one of my mother's countless boxes stacked in my closet, I discovered my Grandpa Turnage's writings. He was my mother's father — the one who walked into the woods behind their house toting his gun each holiday season to shoot down mistletoe for Christmas. I never met Grandpa Turnage, since he died several years before I was born. However, I have seen photographs of this World War I veteran who remained tall and lean throughout his life. His adventurous short stories of growing up in the South remind me of Mark Twain's writings. However, I was most enthralled by his written testimony of faith that he titled "The Little Red Panda." He wrote the following passages in June 1955.

Time: Summer of 1908. I was a nine-year-old boy and had been down with Typhoid Fever for several weeks. The doctor had made his daily call that afternoon. The verdict was bad. Mother and Daddy were concerned and even I could see they were unhappy and more attentive than usual. Someone stayed with me at all times of the day. Both Mother and Daddy were broken of rest. I remember Mother bathing my face and giving me a rubdown. I went into a coma. I don't remember what time of night I was awakened. This light that I had never seen anything like — it came through the house as though the house did not exist. This was made into a snow white stairway as far as I could see and narrowed at the high distance that it extended. The beautiful angels were in the house with snow white wings. Some had blonde hair, some brunette and different colors. The features of them were beautiful young women. They were barefoot. I looked around for Mother and Daddy. I wanted them to see the glorious creatures I was beholding, but I could see that both Mother and Daddy were in a deep sleep. Mother on the bed with me and Daddy on another bed in the room lying across it dressed with only his shoes off. Some voice interrupted as one of these angels approached the bed toward me saying "Not now. Leave him. I have a purpose for him that no other one can fulfill." Then as they looked in my eyes and turned to depart with smiles, I looked far up the stairway and saw my grandfather as an infant. I was just as normal as I had ever been during this experience and thereafter. I called out to Mother and she awoke, and I told her I would not die now. I told her of these things I had seen and heard. She was so happy. She kept that as her secret, and we would talk of it all along through the years of my raising.

To the readers I want to pass these facts to be thought upon when they are spiritually full and want to drink of the glory and beauty that awaits them. Yours may be different, but I say this to be the facts of the only heavenly visitation I have ever experienced. I have refrained from telling this in public testimonials for too many people of this day are ready to shout "Fanatic!"

Out in the plantations in the schools days, old Shagg my dog and I were pals. Everywhere I went old Shagg was at my heels. In the home at night after supper, all the children gathered around the fireside as Mother would sing those old familiar hymns: Leaning on the Everlasting Arms and Amazing Grace. She would thank God before bedtime as we kneeled around her rocker. She would thank God for the blessings of that day and ask that the guardian angels might watch over her family through that night. Yes, I was raised by a Christian mother and an honest daddy. I thank God this day for that. Alas old Shagg died from old age in the late Fall with pennyroyal in bloom in the woods everywhere. We all gathered to pay our last respects to the good old faithful family dog.

It is a life that any normal boy had lived. Yes, the kind of life that we boys have had and the future boys will witness who are blessed to be raised by Christian parents. I recall the night of one of those terrible storms that occurred every year in the part of Georgia where I was raised. . . . The winds were howling and the lightning was striking trees everywhere near our home as torrential rain fell. Seemed that we might all be doomed that night. We could see Mother and Daddy were concerned. Mother drew us all around her and the old rocking chair, and she had a talk with God. We could hear her humble petition as she asked Him to spare us from the fury of that storm as He had the night on the Sea of Galilee. Not too long after, the weather was abating, and we were all hungry and checked with the barns and stock to make sure no harm had been done. Oh the children of my day and this day that don't have praying mothers, my heart bleeds for the youth that don't have Christian backgrounds at their home. A family altar is the answer to both adult delinquency and juvenile delinquency. So many homes I go into that never even have grace at the meals. . . . All through the years and in my early boyhood days we had Sunday School. Out in front of the house under the huge old live oak trees. Then later, Father and other good fathers of that community built a church. . . .

Why I am Baptist. I had a good old-fashioned Methodist grandmother. She was getting on in years when out of a cloudless sky she demanded of her pastor — the Methodist preacher — that she must be immersed in baptism. The whole community was aroused at this decision and turned out in mass to witness an old staunch Methodist be baptized. We went to the Blue Springs where the water was clear as crystal and this song was sung, "Lord I want to be in that number when the Saints go marching home." Then the preacher said, "By your request, I baptize this my sister in the name of our Lord and Jesus Christ." I was looking in Grandmother's eyes as the minister wiped the water from them. She held out her arms and spoke these words: "Glory to God in the highest. Peace in my soul." Several weeks later she died in her sleep and went to that peace.

At 26 years of age I was married in April 1925, and the following Christmas Eve night, I had my first responsibility as a father. Margaret

Delores was born. My wife and I had established the Family Altar in our humble little bungalow. The following May 1926 my mother departed from us and the old plantation. But she had told me not long before that I would be all right and that I had a God who would lead me in all things that I did, and that my life would be mostly a trying life — worldly speaking, but not to disapprove of anything that God laid on my shoulders and that I would be the father of one of God's own servants. She just all but worshipped Margaret as she would look at her as a little baby girl. She would say, "God bless Grandmother's little angel."

In June 1927 we had another charge come to our house: Carolyn Priscilla. We moved from the old plantation in Georgia to Florida. I, having learned the carpentry trade while in the U.S. Army, came to Florida as a carpenter. I have thought of that trade lots as the time passes. I feel that Christ had chosen that trade for me as God had chosen it for His trade. It is a very interesting profession. You are always building, never finished, going from one house to another. So by the grace of God, I am what I am.

Sunday August 1, 1948, Time: Nine o'clock. I was dressing for Sunday School on a beautiful Sabbath morning. The birds were singing so gaily no one could feel any way but happy with all the land of North Florida bathed in sunshine. The fighting had been over and it seemed that the world would soon settle in peace for a season. Ring-Ring. The telephone rang.

Oklahoma City calling Boyd Turnage
    Yes, this is Boyd Turnage speaking (pause)
Margaret has been in an automobile accident (pause).
    Yes sir. This is Guy Bellameny speaking (pause).
Margaret is dead.

Fathers, have you ever got such a telephone message as that? Yes, that moment the very words that Mother had told me 22 years ago flew into my memory. "You have a God who will lead you in all things." Yes I did. Yes, He took hold on me then and there. *I want you to witness for me. You can't witness crying or grieving about the loss of Margaret. I am with you and will be into the uttermost.* I had this thought and answer to that spiritual request, "The Lord giveth and the Lord taketh away. Blessed be the name of the Lord."

Margaret's little bed was bedecked with the many nice graduation presents and her little Red Panda. It was a custom in college that the girls had some kind of doll or animal sit in their pillows as ornaments to the bed. Margaret had chosen the little red panda. Yes, it was hard the next few days waiting for her little mangled body to arrive to Mother and Daddy and our home. By the time it had arrived the skies were pouring out the rain that in a way seemed dark on the broken but brave hearts of this little family.

With her little casket and the many beautiful floral offerings, she lay in state in the little living room as a host of friends and people we had never seen before spent the long hours that night as the rain poured down. No let up in the weather the next morning, the day of the funeral. I feel so grateful to Dr. Courts Redford and for his visit at that time and the humble prayer that he offered up on our behalf. God heard his prayers. One hour before the funeral it appeared that we all would have heavy rain while burying our precious little Margaret. My wife, Carolyn and I all went in a room and locked the door and asked God to kindly hold off the rain until after the funeral. In ten minutes the rain completely stopped and did not rain any more until the people had time to get back home. And then the rain set in again.

Fathers, do you and Mothers pray sincerely? Do you ever lock yourself in a closet or room and talk to God privately? Try that for those hard answered prayers that are worthy to be answered.

Yes, Time heals most wounds but when you think of time it isn't long, even if it be a hundred years.

Time: June 1955. Carolyn is living far away and we don't see her very often as she has her family and duties. I have been totally disabled for over two years now and the active life I have always had I have to slow to a drag now. Mary and I spend most of our time working in the flowers and little vegetable garden I try to raise.

I looked on Margaret's pillow on her little bed some few minutes ago. The little red panda was staring at me with those large glass eyes. It seemed to say to me, "Patience and faith, and to those unsaved, come to Jesus today and take the water of life freely." Margaret would say, "Come," but the little red panda can't talk and say, "Come." Margaret can't say, "Come" to you, but her works and the life she lived — and other means that we hope to establish — can say, "Come" and with this testimonial and memoriam to Margaret, if purchased and read by you, may be the voice of the little red panda and Margaret that causes you to come to the Lord. For the fields are white, and the laborers are few.

I have tried in my feeble way to portray in this little story the need of the spiritual foundation that is needed in the homes of today. I have tried to explain the sorrows that can be counted blessings in this; I have not put myself up as holier than thou, but have shown through facts that it pays to be raised by Christian parents with family altars and music and song. I believe that this is the only answer to the huge giant that we are calling juvenile delinquency, and it is from parental neglect. I believe that a Christian home is the answer to the atom bombs and World Peace. I have tried in this little article to be of comfort to those that can't adjust to the loss of a loved one. I have pointed them to the answer. I, being one of the smallest laymen, in my humble way to God, want to leave this message to this generation. And as they read this little pamphlet, it will help them prepare for the service of our Lord and Savior Jesus Christ.

Boyd Turnage

I treasure these yellowed pages typed by my grandfather nearly six decades ago. What a gift to have a written record of my grandfather's testimony of faith and a narrative of his near death experience. Sharing stories were the tangible handles that he had found to help guide him through his grief. And on a side note, the little red panda that I found tucked away inside a separate box sits on my desk as I write this book. Actually, the little red panda has faded into a little pink panda through the decades. Nevertheless, this precious stuffed animal has become my little mascot, a tangible connection to my grandfather's foundation of lasting faith.

Grandpa Turnage died before my mother's first book was ever published. Had he lived, I am sure that he would have realized that he was the father of two of God's own servants. My mother's unique word pictures have provided tangible handles for thousands of readers to better understand intangible concepts of Christianity. Her poetic parables — as I like to describe them — are practical teaching tools for walking and living by faith and for feeling the love and comfort of the Lord.

A few years after my dad's death, my mother established the Margaret Turnage Student Missions Scholarship Fund at Palm Beach Atlantic University. PBAU students have been able to use this scholarship to help fund their mission trips overseas. Since my mother's death, the university continues to forward letters written by students sharing their experiences overseas and thanking the family for supporting this special fund. Isn't God amazing how His ultimate will for my Aunt Margaret's life was achieved? Yes, she became and continues to be an overseas missionary to multiple countries across the world through college students who hear her story and receive funds to travel to these foreign lands and share the hope that is found in Christ.

Writing this book has become my final handle on grief. Throughout my personal journey, however, I discovered other handles too. Here are my suggestions.

COMPLETE AN UNFINISHED PROJECT
OR UNFULFILLED DREAM

One handle that I found to be especially helpful was to complete something that my parents didn't have a chance to finish while on Earth. For my dad that was to finish researching the family tree with those Revolutionary War patriots he had always heard about growing up but had never officially documented. During retirement, he had planned to conduct further research so he could provide the necessary documentation to join National Society of the Sons of the American Revolution (NSSAR) as a means to honor his forefathers who had fought for America's freedom as a nascent country. I think this was particularly important to my dad since he was a veteran of WWII and his father was a veteran of WWI. Each Veterans Day, my dad loved to sing the patriotic songs as he beamed with pride knowing that each previous generation had a veteran who had served our country. As a tribute to my father, I tediously documented his ancestral bloodline that officially tied him via birth records, last will and testaments, and published articles to several patriots of the Revolutionary War. I completed his unfinished task on Earth by becoming a member of the National Society of the Daughters of the American Revolution (NSDAR) to honor his memory.

My mother's unfinished task was promoting her book *When Grief Is Your Constant Companion: God's Grace for a Woman's Heartache.* In anticipation of the book signings and possible speaking engagements, my mother had purchased a few lovely dresses and even a whole line of makeup. She hardly ever spent money on herself, especially since my dad had passed away. She was determined to look her best while doing her best to market the book for New Hope. However, she was diagnosed with a terminal illness at the same time her new book was released. During one of my visits to Florida, we walked into her closet so she could show me the outfits she had purchased. Sliding a few coat hangers to the side, she lifted a lovely dress and said, "This is what I was planning to wear to my first book signing, but I've relinquished all my dreams for promoting the book." She was neither resentful nor wistful, but rather accepting of reality. "And I'd like for you to take all of that expensive makeup that I splurged on," Mother laughed. "What was I even thinking?"

My mother never had an official book signing to launch her book on grief. However, she signed each copy that New Hope had given her in advance. What my mother inscribed inside my copy of her book would be her final written communication to me.

To Meg, my beloved daughter, whose encouragement kept me pursuing my dream to find a publisher for this book. I love you dearly. Follow your dreams too. I'll be cheering you on!

Love, Mother
Dec 16, 2002

On June 27, 2003 — on what would have been my mother's 76th birthday — I hosted a book signing party at a local Barnes and Noble. Friends from church and the community came to celebrate my mother's life and enjoy a piece of the birthday cake I brought along. Everyone was so gracious to purchase a book, the proceeds of which were directed to help fund The Margaret Turnage Student Missionary Scholarship Fund. I signed my mother's books on her behalf and read aloud a few of her poems.

Yet, one important unfinished task remained, and I knew what that task was the moment I found my Aunt Margaret's memorial book in one of the boxes. With reverence and care, I turned each delicate page. Toward the back of the book were some newspaper clippings, and I discovered the name of the driver and the town in which he lived. The memory of my mother sharing her regret of not ever reaching out to speak with the driver of the car rushed into my mind. I knew what I had to do.

I picked up the phone and called the church that had been mentioned in the article. The church secretary answered the phone, and I asked if she knew how I could contact this person. She paused and said, "Oh. I am so sorry. He was the pastor, but he just passed away a month ago." I could hardly breathe. Hadn't I found this phone number for a purpose? And now I faced a closed door.

Then the church secretary said, "But why don't I give you the name and number of his widow?" Immediately, I had sudden stage fright and called my brother Claude before we tried to reach the widow. As the woman's phone rang, my stomach twisted and my mind raced with frightening thoughts. *What if she didn't even know about my Aunt Margaret? Will she be offended by our call?* Soon, the widow answered, and I introduced myself and my brother. I told her the words my mother had wanted to share with her husband many years ago — that she was at peace. I thought about the words transcribed from my mother's speech recorded in the 1970s: *You know within this larger context of the will of God, no human circumstance or tragic event is ever beyond the redemptive power of God. As I expectantly abide in God's ongoing will, he can work creatively for good in every situation and help me keep on growing as I reach up to him and out to others.*

The widow then told my brother and me that she remembered our Aunt Margaret. In fact, it was Margaret, she told us, who invited her to get involved in the church again. She said that her husband had felt such remorse and guilt about the accident, but God had seen him through this difficulty. She told us that he had been a wonderful pastor who had led many people to Christ through the years. We ended the phone call with a prayer that Claude led. We thanked God for the wonderful legacy of my Aunt Margaret and for the impact she had and still has on so many people's lives. We thanked God for the blessing of being brought together to remember our loved ones and to praise Him. Only God could have orchestrated this incredible reunion. I later sent a copy of *When Grief Is Your Constant Companion* to this kind woman. What a perfect circle of faith that the widow of the driver that accidentally killed my Aunt Margaret would find comfort through the pages of my mother's final book. I call that "recycled grace."

Completing something my mother had left unfinished didn't provide closure, but it did bring comfort through the presence of God's grace.

CREATE NEW TRADITIONS

Special days and holidays can be very difficult as you mark these occasions without your loved one's presence. After becoming an adult orphan in 2003, I started a new tradition for Christmas. Each year, I purchase a Christmas cross ornament to hang on the tree as a tangible reminder that I grieve for my loved ones and friends with faith. Because of Christ's resurrection three days after He died upon a tree that was His cross, we know that death is not the end of life, but rather the beginning of eternal life for those who love and trust Him. As I hang each Christmas cross, I remember a special memory of those loved ones who have passed. After all the Christmas cross ornaments are fastened securely onto the branches, I close my eyes and pray, thanking God for my loving parents and for their significant influence in my life.

While hanging my eighth Christmas cross ornament on the tree in 2010, I also thought about my brother, Randy, who had passed away on December 2 only a few weeks prior. Through my tears I smiled as I thought, "This will be his first Christmas in heaven with my parents."

This new tradition of Christmas cross ornaments has brought comfort along with a tangible way to remember those who have passed. At the beginning of December, I try to recall those friends of mine who lost loved ones that year. I then order Christmas cross ornaments to send to these friends along with a note that explains my new tradition. Giving a Christmas cross ornament has become a way for me to comfort others from the comfort I have received from God.

My mother includes this touching poem from an unknown author in her book on grief.

BECOMING A COMFORTER

The flash that struck thy tree — no more
To shelter thee — lets heaven's blue floor
Shine where it never shone before.
The cry wrung from thy spirit's pain
May echo in some far-off plain,
And guide a wanderer home again.
— AUTHOR UNKNOWN

I hope you have found comfort in these special family stories, testimonies, and traditions that I shared with you. These "helping handles" have enabled me to grasp onto something tangible while stumbling in the dark along grief's path and tripping over the intensity of intangible emotions. With God's help, you, too, will discover your own unique "helping handles" and then in turn reach out to others and help comfort them.

Recently, a dear friend's father passed away, and she joined the growing population of adult orphans. Upon hearing the sad news, I immediately sent an email to her since she lives in London. (Perhaps instead I should have sent a handwritten letter.) This is an excerpt of the email I wrote to comfort her.

I want to comfort you and offer reassurance as you begin your journey as an adult orphan. Embrace the waves of grief that surprise you with their intensity at times as a form of cleansing that washes through your innermost being. It has been so emotional to write my book that is due in three weeks about the journey of grief. I just found letters in a box that provided a glimpse into who my parents were. I cried for days perpetuated I am sure by the fact that Melissa leaves our home on Monday for her journey as a young adult in college. The grown up vision often collides with the inner child's version. We gain a deeper appreciation and even acceptance of our parents, life and the genuine legacy that we now carry with us. Your parents truly loved you, May and were so proud of you! How blessed you are! As wisdom and truth cleanses our heart with tears, we at last discover a settled peace that affirms our faith and provides sustenance for the journey ahead to face without fear the changes as we discover deeper meaning and individual purpose. May, you are such an incredible person with great strengths and great purpose.

Be comforted and encouraged through your vision of faith that God remains constant even in the midst of change. And embrace my father's favorite Bible verse inscribed on his tombstone: Isaiah 43:19. So May, look for the new things that God is doing in your life! He is making a way in the wilderness and rivers in the desert.

I am here for you, dear friend and am praying for you.

Consider yourself hugged!

Meg

Comfort

"In my Father's house are many mansions: if it were not so, I would have told you. I go to prepare a place for you. And if I go and prepare a place for you, I will come again, and receive you unto myself; that where I am, there ye may be also." JOHN 14:2 3

"Eye hath not seen, nor ear heard . . . the things which God hath prepared for them that love him." 1 CORINTHIANS 2:9

"And Jesus said unto him, Verily I say unto thee, Today shalt thou be with me in paradise." LUKE 23:43

"And God shall wipe away all tears from their eyes." Revelation 7:17

"A man's gift maketh room for him." PROVERBS 18:16

"Go home to thy friends, and tell them how great things the Lord hath done for thee, and hath had compassion on thee." MARK 5:19

COUNSEL

- In your dark time of despair, I encourage you to pray that God will open the eyes of your heart so that you can see Christ high and exalted in all His glory and splendor (read Isaiah 6:1–4). As you see Christ, also know your loved one is with Him. What comfort! God is the God of the living, not the dead. Your loved one is alive and Jesus has him or her with Him at the throne this very moment (John 14:1–3; Revelation 3:21).

  What is Jesus doing on the throne? The Bible teaches that He is interceding "night and day" for you, me, and other brothers and sisters who remain on this earth (Romans 8:34; Hebrews 7:25). Just think, your loved one is with Jesus as He is calling out your name to God! I am increasingly convinced people in heaven are much more aware of our lives than perhaps we have imagined. The fact that your loved one is hearing Christ intercede for you leads me to believe he or she knows some of what is going on in your life.

  Additionally, Scriptures teach there is much joy in the presence of God's angels over one sinner who repents (Luke 15:8–10). The Bible doesn't say the angels rejoice, but those in the presence of the angels rejoice. It appears to me that our loved ones with Christ are rejoicing in the presence of angels over men and women, boys and girls who are being saved on this earth. Moses and Elijah were also granted to know, to some extent, what was happening on the earth as they talked with Jesus about things that were about to happen (Luke 9:28–31).

  Also, the Bible hints that departed Christians know of their existence, the fate of the wicked, that they will be rewarded, all while they are told to wait patiently until the events on the earth are fulfilled (Luke 23:43; 2 Corinthians 5:8; Philippians 1:23; Revelation 6:9–11). In short, I am convinced that your loved one is part of a great cloud of witnesses that is more aware of you than you realize. I believe he or she is encouraging you to finish the race God has placed before you (see Hebrews 12:1–2).

Therefore, do not lose heart for soon and very soon you, as a follower of Jesus Christ, will be with your Savior and those believers who have gone before you. Let this great news bring peace and comfort to your weary soul and provide strength for you to finish your life for the glory of God. *Pastor Rob Jackson, Senior Pastor of Central Baptist Church in Decatur, Alabama*

Chronicling

What are some helping handles that I should consider?

Are there some things that I can do to help others? Who needs my help and what needs to be done?

Chapter 10
Footprints of Faith

"Meg, this is Elaine. I'm so sorry to call you with this news, but Randy died today."

I was in the kitchen when my sister-in-law called on December 2, 2010. She went on to explain that my 53-year-old brother had suffered a massive heart attack while feeding a stray cat on the back deck of their house. He loved animals. Randy always had a tender place in his heart for others who needed a little extra care or direction in life.

Randy's death was like déjà vu 20 years after my dad's sudden death in Paris. After speaking with Elaine, I sobbed. I mourned the death of my brother, and I also grieved for the past years during which we had drifted apart. We had not seen each other since my mother's funeral in April 2003. Each year Randy would call me on my birthday, and I am grateful that he reached out to me in March 2010. It was Spring Break when he called around 8:30 P.M. Our conversation was fairly brief. He said he wanted to wish me a happy birthday and let me know that he was doing fine — completely clean and sober. He said he was a different person now. I told him that I loved him and had tried to call him on his birthday, Christmas, and many other times, too, throughout these years. He told me that he just needed some time and to be patient. This was our last conversation.

Once again, my clutter became a blessing. While doing a little fall cleaning during October 2010, I found the Christmas 2009 gift cards for Randy and Elaine that I had forgotten to mail. After writing a brief note of apology on the outside for the delayed mailing, I drove to the post office. After the funeral when we all had time to visit, Elaine told me that Randy had chuckled to himself when Christmas arrived in October: "What is Meg thinking? Has she lost her mind? Christmas is months away." Elaine said that they had used one of the gift cards to take some special friends out to dinner. My late — or rather early — Christmas gift had provided a happy celebration over a meal, and that brings me comfort. In the cemetery, Elaine shared the details of what had precipitated the miraculous change in Randy's life that he had alluded to during my birthday phone call from him. I promise to share this inexplicable miracle with you later in this chapter. However, for you to fully understand and appreciate Randy's new beginning, I must first provide the proper framework of his past and place it alongside my mother's foundation of faith. My mother's prayers for Randy would at last be answered in God's timing, and her lasting legacy of prayer would leave an indelible mark of faith that no one will ever be able to wash away.

Clipped inside her spiral bound journal entitled *The Prayer Pilgrimage of Carolyn Rhea,* I found a handwritten note entitled *Leaving a Legacy.* I'm not sure of the exact timing in which she wrote it — sometime after my father's death in 1990. My mother was carefully contemplating her legacy — a great lesson for all of us. Have we thought about how we want to be thought about? If you were to ask a close friend or family member, what would he or she say that your legacy is? This is what my mother wrote.

Leaving a Legacy

Claude's legacy of love, laughter, great faith, encouragement, joy, vision, courage (illness) music.

My legacy of love, prayer(?) creativity, simplicity (frugality) common-sense

My mother's greatest legacy is that of prayer. Prayer was the centerpiece of her life. I always remember her as a prayer warrior who would wake up at 5 A.M. each morning to read her Bible and pray. I must confess that I never have been a morning person. She wrote two books on prayer: *Come Pray With Me* and *My Heart Kneels, Too,* in addition to a study guide *When You Pray.*

My mother taught me how to pray at a very young age. I still have the vivid memories of her bringing a remnant of indoor carpet into my bedroom. "Look, Meg. You now have a prayer mat." We kept my prayer mat beneath my bed, and each night my mother and I would kneel on our prayer mats and talk to God. Apparently I felt so comfortable talking to God that I would even say in the middle of a prayer, "Oh, God, please erase that last thing I just said."

Prayer is a powerful and personal mode of communication with God, an incredible grace gift enabling us to connect with our heavenly Father. I love His promise in Jeremiah 33:3: "Call unto me and I will answer thee, and shew thee great and mighty things, which thou knowest not."

My mother defined prayer as the "doorway to God" and even writes about this concept using me as an illustration.

Doorway to God

Our home has a screened back porch which opens out from the family room and kitchen. Our two-year-old daughter is content to stay there for several hours at a time, playing with her sandbox, some large wooden blocks, and an assortment of other toys.

I always latch the screen door leading into the backyard so that she cannot slip out. Knowing that she is comparatively safe and secure, I can go about my work in the kitchen and glance through the double windows over the sink to watch her at play.

Sometimes, my daughter feels quite independent and will run up and slam the door between the porch and the family room, shutting herself off from me. How smug and independent she looks playing on the porch alone, completely unaware that I am still watching her through the kitchen windows.

Sometimes, while the door is still closed, she will abruptly stop what she is doing as if she suddenly feels an acute need for "Mommy" and realizes that the door is closed between us. Quickly she will run to the door (which she herself has closed), open it and rush in to me.

Are we not like that with God? We know, of course, that God is really omnipresent. He is with us at all times. We know that His love and care surround us, and yet, feeling quite independent, we close ourselves off from Him and go about our work and play. God does not invade our privacy or our freedom. Suddenly, though, there comes an acute awareness that we need the comforting assurance of His presence. Dropping everything, we turn the knob and step through the doorway of prayer into his presence, realizing only then how very near he had been all the time, how tenderly he had been watching over us.

We ourselves are the ones who shut God out of our lives. Through Christ, God has left the door open forever for us to come freely into his presence; yet we choose so often to close the door between us. We feel so smug and independent, so self-sufficient, when in reality we are utterly dependent upon God's great love and care.

Prayer, then, is the doorway to God. On our part, it is a conscious opening unto God. Through it we step into the presence of Almighty God.[2]

I loved my mother's prayer parables — perhaps we should call them "prayer"ables. Mother shared such vivid word pictures that explained otherwise complicated concepts. I was thrilled to discover a devotional video she had filmed in 1986 — only four years before my dad's death. In an earlier chapter I shared her first two devotionals about life being a series of moves and the heartwarming story about mistletoe at Christmas. In the final video segment, my mother shares her legacy — her thoughts and illustrations on intercessory prayer.

Have you ever been on the receiving end of intercessory prayer? If so, did you sense that someone was praying for you personally with such power that you could feel the impact of that prayer in your life?

I've had such an experience. A number of years ago my husband was in the hospital for cancer surgery. The doctors gave him little hope for recovering. Friends prayed earnestly for us. I penned my thoughts about that experience in my book *My Heart Kneels Too*.

INVISIBLE SEESAW

I felt that someone prayed for me,
For there came an inner awareness
That someone cared enough to send through God
Remembrance of my heavy burden and my special need of Him
It was as if God's mercy
Transformed that prayer into an invisible seesaw
Which lifted me while the weight of my burden
Rested briefly on the other end.
And with the lightened load, my tenseness
Thawed in the warm therapy of love and care
And new strength came now that I was more relaxed and trusting.
I knew that somewhere someone had prayed for me.[3]

I recognized the fact that I had been on the receiving end of God's prayer promise in James 5:16: "The effectual fervent prayer of a righteous man availeth much."

Within God's will and purpose my husband lived and I, too, received the strength that I needed for my own burdens of helping him during his recovery, and of taking care of our two young sons — one not quite four years old at the time and the other not quite two.

Those sons a few years later taught me a valuable lesson about prayer. We'd moved to Texas. One day I saw them outside holding a magnifying glass over a piece of paper. You can imagine what happened in that blazing Texas sun. I saw a spiritual simile:

INTENSIFIED

Impartially, the sun shines alike on everyone.
(So does God's loving care!)
Yet those rays can be intensified
With a simple magnifying glass,
And that which is held beneath
Feels greater warmth.
So each day I place myself and others
'Neath God's magnifying glass of prayer
That we might feel in greater measure
His Love and Strength and Joy.[4]

Somehow the analogy of a magnifying glass encouraged me to become an intercessor to pray earnestly for my family and loved ones, for my friends, my neighbors, my church, my community, my country and yes, my world.

Do you remember the telecommunications satellite called Telstar? It was the inspiration for this thought about prayer.

TELSTAR

When I pray
For someone around the world,
Does he know?
Is it worth the worry spent?
Can it really help?
If human hands have fashioned
Telstar out in space
To bounce again to Earth
The words and image sent across the seas,
Surely God
Can redirect my little prayer
Into that life
For whom I pray
And fuse with it
His wondrous love and care.[5]

The ministry of intercession takes time and self discipline. Could it be that perhaps you have time in your life now that you could devote to intercessory prayer? Would you be willing to do so?

It also requires faith. Faith in God's marvelous promises about prayer and faith to appropriate in your own prayer life. These prayer promises such as "the fervent effectual prayer of a righteous man [or woman] shall availeth much" James 5:16; and Christ's incredible promise when he said, "And whatsoever ye shall ask in my name, that will I do, that the Father may be glorified in the Son" (John 14:13). And these words that he said, "All things whatsoever ye shall ask in my name, believing he shall receive."

Are you willing to become an intercessor?

Hearing and seeing my mother ask this question as she stared into the camera jolted my inner being. Are you willing to become an intercessor? I searched within myself and asked if I have the necessary self-discipline and time in my life right now. The honest answer to that question is "Not right now." But why not? Why does my soul struggle with my response? I find myself rationalizing. "But, God, don't I have huge responsibilities for family and home, writing deadlines, Kitchen Chat (my Internet radio show), Pearl Girls, charitable board responsibilities — and everything else?" As I write these excuses, I hear God's still, small voice within my spirit, "Yes, child, and that's why it is even more important that you make the time to pray. Use this grace gift I have given you to build a closer relationship with Me and with those for whom you pray. Remember, my daughter, you will have even more time for your earthly commitments when your life is fully committed to Me through prayer. I know the plans I have for you."

Right this moment, I am going to stop writing and pray for you. This time my "prayer mat" will be a "prayer pillow" — since my middle-aged knees need a bit more padding these days. Although we might not know each other, we both know well the emotions of grief. Why don't you take this moment and pray too? Call out to God. Cry out to God. Give God the heaviness of your heart. He loves you so much that He gave you Jesus, His only Son, as a gift of grace to you. Through Christ we have eternal life, and although the sorrow of the "meanwhile" is difficult now, please remember that it is only temporary.

(Please take a few moments here and pray.)

As promised, I knelt on my prayer pillow and prayed for you, dear reader, even though I do not know your name or your specific sorrow. I hope you feel lifted on the invisible seesaw and that your grief doesn't feel quite as heavy right now. And I encourage you to keep on praying.

Oh, and I would like for God to please erase what I said before about not having time right now in my life. I would like officially to change my answer to a "yes" in response to my mother's question, "Are you willing to become an intercessor?" Although I will never have my mother's self-discipline or her penchant for prayer during the early morning hours, I do hope that I will have her heart for prayer and her fervent faith that "with God all things are possible" (Matthew 19:26).

At this point, you might be asking, "Do you want to invest time in praying? Does it really work?" Without hesitation, I can answer that question with a resounding "Yes." I can personally attest to the power of prayer. In one instance, my life was saved through an obedient and immediate act of intercessory prayer, and in another instance, my brother Randy's life was saved and changed after countless years and hours of intercessory prayer.

At age 19, I had my tonsils removed after suffering from too many cases of tonsillitis further complicated by bronchitis and severe sinus infections. My parents brought me to the hospital for what was supposed to be a routine surgical procedure with a quick overnight stay. (This was before outpatient surgeries.) All was going well with the tonsillectomy until I became the unusual case that my experienced doctor had always read about in text books but had never encountered after decades of surgeries. He later explained to me that blood is attracted to infection and that an artery had re-routed itself directly into my left tonsil. When he surgically removed this tonsil, he accidentally severed the artery, and I almost bled to death. Nurses summoned a doctor in the adjacent operating room to rush to my surgeon's aid to help cauterize the artery and stabilize my condition. I even had to have an emergency transfusion due to the excessive loss of blood. Meanwhile, my parents wondered why I was in surgery beyond the typical one-hour mark. I actually found a note my mom had written about my tonsillectomy.

Notes 1982

Meg — tonsils & adenoids out in Jan. 1982. Dr. accidentally cut an artery in her throat. She stayed in the hospital 6 days. I was in the process of grading *mid-term exams and giving semester grades at Mtn. Brook High School. Also in the process of packing to move to Florida.*

My doctor was very kind, and he constantly came to my hospital room during those six days to personally make sure I was OK. The experience really must have frightened him. We all knew, however that this would have happened no matter who the surgeon was, and I am grateful for his clear thinking and years of experience. I would soon realize, however that it wasn't only the doctor's hands and head that affected my life that day.

While visiting me in my hospital room the day after my tonsillectomy, my parents shared an incredible story. Earlier that morning, my dad had received a call from one of his evangelist friends. My dad said this friend called him at work and urgently asked, "Is everything OK? I was the guest speaker at a church in Michigan, and the Holy Spirit put a heavy need upon my heart to pray for your family. I stopped preaching and asked the congregation to join me in prayer for the Claude Rhea family." This evangelist heeded the Holy Spirit and led the congregation in an impromptu intercessory prayer meeting. My dad asked his friend if he remembered what time he had felt this pressing need to pray. They both soon realized that this prayer took place at the exact time I was facing life-threatening complications during my tonsillectomy. I was the recipient of intercessory prayer! I wish that I had asked my dad for the name of the evangelist who had prayed for me. I would like to thank that righteous man for his fervent and effectual prayer!

The second life-changing example of intercessory prayer involved my brother, Randy. He was a wonderful person who was led astray by peer pressure. With a pre-existing disposition to addiction, Randy struggled with drugs and alcohol almost his entire life. As a rebellious teenager, Randy constantly ran away from home. My mother blamed herself for my brother's actions and decisions in life. However, I never knew the full extent of her guilt until I read the pages of her journal. Randy was always a kind and loving big brother, and I knew that he would find his purposed path in life even after he dropped out of high school. He was very intelligent, creative, and hardworking and worked hard to earn his GED. My parents constantly reached out to him and prayed for him. I shall never forget God's timing in answering one of their prayers for Randy. My mother writes about that miraculous moment in her book *Come Pray with Me*.

THE PRODIGAL RETURNS

My husband and I helped organize a prayer group in our church. It was one of several electives open to adults on Wednesday evening.

In attendance our prayer group ranged from 5 to 12. During those weeks we learned to open up to each other and to pray together. We gave regular, sustained, intercessory prayer support for our pastor and church staff, the church family, the church program of activities, Sunday school teachers, leaders in the church, the young people, and each other.

It came at a time of great personal need in my husband's life and mine. Our younger son, still in his teens, had rebelliously run away from home. For a while, I wallowed in guilt, self-pity, and anguish . . .

Had there been general church family prayer meetings at the time, I would probably have made an unspoken prayer request. Within the small prayer group, however, I was able to open up and share something of my deep need with the others. How they supported us in prayer! Week after week in the prayer group and day after day in their private prayers they prayed both for our son Randy and for us. Their prayers helped sustain us through the experience.

One Wednesday evening our group had just finished praying. Again they had prayed for Randy and for us. There was a noise at the door of the prayer room, an embarrassed cough, and a rather subdued voice said, "Mother . . ."

Our prodigal son had returned — dirty and disheveled — seemingly drawn homeward and churchward by the magnet of intercessory prayer!

You may explain it as you wish, but I believe Randy's return from the "far country" was a part of the continuing miracle of intercessory prayer.

Some months later our returned son was penning his thoughts in poetry. The closing line of one of his poems posed a poignant and searching question: "Am I just one of God's forgotten thoughts?"

No! No one is a "forgotten thought" of God! But often the comforting reassurance comes through the channel of the intercessory prayers of Christian friends.[6]

I cry each time I read Randy's question: "Am I just one of God's forgotten thoughts?" In his early 20s, Randy found true love with his soul mate and wonderful wife, Elaine. She was a firm foundation of faith throughout their marriage of 30 years and patiently endured and prayed for Randy's continuous struggles with addiction. My mother loved Elaine like a daughter.

For decades, my mother continued to pray for Randy as evidenced by her notes and markings within the margins of her Bible and on the pages of devotional books. Mother intentionally wrote Randy's name by God's promises and underlined passages. One phrase especially stood out to me that my mother had underlined on page 121 in her copy of *Streams in the Desert*: "It takes God time to answer prayer." She wrote Randy '95, Randy '96, Randy '97, Randy 1998!!! Randy 2000! 2001 — inked markings of her fervent faith and constant prayers for him. I always knew that my mother carried a heavy burden of guilt about Randy, and she often expressed this concern to me. However, upon reading an entry in her personal journal, I better understand the weight of her guilt.

Randy is into drugs and alcohol again. Father, Thy will be done in these circumstances. I have failed him all of his life by not giving him enough love and affirmation and self-esteem and not letting him suffer the consequences of his wrong choices. Please forgive me, Lord. The battle is God's!!! April 26, 1997

I can honestly say that I do not recall my mother's not giving Randy enough love and affirmation. She equally loved each of her children. It's heartbreaking for any parent to feel that he or she has failed a child. We all do the best that we can to love, protect, nurture and guide our children. The reality is that we are human and yes, as parents we do make mistakes — and as adults we must take responsibilities for those mistakes. Throughout the course of motherhood, I have apologized many times to my daughters. No one is a perfect parent. As my mother always said, we must "speak the truth with love" and be patient.

I found my mother's touching tribute to Randy stashed within her many papers. What a treasured reminder this is for parents, grandparents, aunts, and uncles to put into writing the attributes of a loved one and to share it with that person.

MY BELOVED SON RANDY
(a few of his many wonderful qualities)
GENEROUS
Using his dollar to treat the neighborhood kids to popsicles!
ENTERPRISING
Finding colorful little gourds growing in the neighborhood and selling them to neighbors who were delighted to buy them.
TRUSTING
At 16 months, waving bye-bye to his father and me as he was rolled into the operating room for a tonsillectomy.
POETIC
Seeing God's world with fresh insight and expressing those thoughts memorably.
LOVING
Tender, caring, loving toward me and his father, Grandma, Chee Chee and Pappy, C3, Meg and most of all (as it should be!) toward his beloved wife Elaine (and loving toward her family too).
DETERMINED
To finish his GED and to pass the courses he started at Junior College.

RESPONSIBLE

Hard-working, using his gift of memorizing parts to become an outstanding warehouse supervisor.

SKILLED AT FISHING

Catching fish even at an early age! Still catching fish and enjoying the recreation of fishing and the joy of sharing fish with family and friends.

MUSICAL

Playing the mandolin, taking piano and violin lessons.

SPIRITUAL

Experiencing a deep sense of God's love,

With child-like faith, trusting Christ as his own personal Savior,

An unashamed Christian who is wanting to keep on growing spiritually (Your father loved the wonderful prayer you prayed for him before surgery at Duke University Hospital).

My mother's written prayers reflect her persistent belief that God would heal Randy from the addictions that had become insurmountable roadblocks to His divine path for my brother. These fervent prayers of a righteous mother for her wayward son can serve as templates for our own written petitions to the Lord. My mother truly prays with expectancy.

June 2, 1997

Randy is in jail. Father, the battle is Yours.

Thank you Lord for the contract on the sale of the house. Thank you for sending the dove again.

June 3, 1997

Thank you Father, for letting Randy go to jail to experience what prison is really like. You were with him, using it for good. Thank you for this _new beginning_.

Love,

Your daughter, Carolyn

July 27, 1997

Randy slipped again, but there is hope in God's unfailing love. The battle is not yours, but God's. 2 Chron. 20:15

My mother's prayers for Randy remained constant. She wrote her heartfelt intercessions throughout the pages of her two favorite daily devotional books: *Streams in the Desert* and *My Utmost for His Highest*. Here is a sampling of her written prayers penned along the margins of dog-eared and highlighted pages from 1992 to 2002:

God's vision for Randy not my vision! Randy's life!!
You are the God of the Impossible!!
Father, please help me strengthen Randy's hand in Thee;
What a difference in Randy's life now! I praise You, God! Thank You, Jesus Christ, our Savior!
Lord, make Randy whole. Wholeness of body, mind, & spirit.
But there is God!

My mother often ended our conversations by saying, "But there is God!" whenever we discussed her concerns about Randy. She had surrendered the impossible to God, knowing that indeed "All things are possible with God."

During the funeral, the pastor kept talking about Randy's changed life. Standing at the altar, the pastor told friends and family members present that God had completely transformed Randy. He was not the same person at the end of his life that we knew him to be growing up. At age 46, Randy became a new person in Christ. He had quit rebelling and embraced his new roles as a lay minister and director of a men's choral group at the church. And he had become in the truest sense, "a fisher of men," patiently teaching numerous troubled teen boys and men with broken lives how to fish. Sitting in a small boat and surrounded by water, Randy spent hours counseling and encouraging these boys and men. They knew that Randy was authentic in his faith and that he had most likely experienced whatever it was that the individual was going through at the moment. There in the stillness of a lake or on the slope of a riverbank, Randy fished, shared his testimony, and invited these grieving souls to experience God's gentle grace and love.

My brother, Randy, always was quite the fisherman. I must confess that I have queasy childhood memories of fish smells, severed fish heads, and wiggly worms impaled upon a hook. Needless to say, I never embraced this pastime. Randy once offered to teach me how to scale a fish, but I felt ill. Growing up, Randy longed to spend his free time on a riverbank or in a boat on a lake, casting the line, patiently waiting and then reeling in the catch. Somehow he always knew where the fish were, even if no one else in his party was catching anything.

Elaine said that during the first week of June 2010, only six months before Randy passed, he spent a long day fishing alone at the lake in a nearby camp. As evening approached, Randy felt prompted to look up at the sky and to take pictures of the clouds with his camera phone. When he returned home, he told Elaine about the inner prompting he had experienced to look up and photograph the clouds. He then handed the phone to her.

"Have you looked at this?" Elaine asked Randy with a rushed excitement in her voice. Immediately, they both saw it — the face — an angel in the clouds.

Elaine told me that this urgent nudge to take the photograph had affected Randy in a deep way. Elaine said that that they never really talked about it again. The trajectory of his life path had taken a huge detour over the past seven years. Perhaps in that quiet moment of seeing an angel's face in the clouds, he was reminded of his own miracle. Words could never accurately articulate what had transformed within his inner soul.

After my mother's death in 2003, Randy's life spiraled downward. He had battled drugs and alcohol throughout his life.

Like an overpowering magnetic field force, his addictions pulled him into the abyss as he tried to numb the guilt and grief through a quick fix of cocaine, marijuana, narcotics, and the liquid morphine prescribed to reduce the pain from a leg wound that wouldn't heal. His body was broken, and his heart was probably broken, too, so soon after Mother's death.

According to Elaine, Randy really hit rock bottom in 2004. "Cocaine always caused him to become violent," she explained. "After working the third shift, he came home early that morning and lunged for me. I called the police, and they made him leave. He went back to work and called me to apologize. We both knew that we couldn't continue down this path." Randy needed help and one of Elaine's stipulations was for him to go to rehab where a doctor could help him get off the drugs. Randy gave his permission to do whatever was necessary, but at that time Elaine couldn't find anyone that could help him.

During the drug withdrawal period, Randy ran a fever and started to cry. That was always a typical pattern for him in the coming down period from prior drug episodes, but Elaine said this time it was different. He kept crying and saying that he should just kill himself. Elaine at first thought he would just get over it, but this downward spiral lasted several days. Randy kept saying, "My leg, my life, everything is a mess. I might as well just die." He quickly sank into a deep depression.

For the next four nights, Randy was put on suicide watch and placed in a private part of a hospital where a nurse was assigned to stay with him at all times. He wouldn't talk. Then, as the doctors started the drug weaning process, Randy yelled and screamed. Elaine would come and go to visit him, but she just couldn't take it any more. Everything looked hopeless. Randy wasn't making any progress. That fourth night when she left his hospital, Elaine decided that she wouldn't come back. But God had other plans.

At three o'clock the next morning, the Lord woke up Elaine

and said, "Get up, get dressed and go to the hospital." She ignored this urgent tug at her spirit, pulled a pillow around her ears and rolled onto her side. This time, the Lord spoke with a louder voice, "Elaine, get up now, get dressed and go to the hospital." This time she obeyed. At around five in the morning, Elaine walked into Randy's hospital room. The curtains were open, and Randy was sitting up in bed smiling.

"Where's the nurse?" Elaine asked.

"I've had an experience, and I need to tell you," Randy insisted. "At about three o'clock this morning, the Lord stood right here at the end of my bed. Jesus himself. I know it was Jesus. He told me, 'Randy, you have a choice. You can continue the lifestyle you're living and die,'" Randy paused and looked over at Elaine, "And I know that meant I would die really soon. 'Or,' Jesus said, 'you can change your life to serve me. Make the choice right now.'" And Randy did.

That same day, Elaine took Randy back home. He was released from suicide watch, released from the hospital and at last released from the permanent prison of his addiction. For the remaining years of his life, Randy never took any drugs, alcohol, or even cigarettes. Doctors and nurses at the hospital were very shocked at Randy's transformation. That miracle in Randy's life took place in May 2004.

My mother's prayers were at last answered in the most spectacular way. In my heart, I like to imagine that my mother started praying for Randy in heaven the second she arrived by personally petitioning the Lord at His throne. Reading the passage and my mother's markings from the April 9 daily devotion in *My Utmost for His Highest* now brings me such inexplicable joy and peace especially after Elaine shared Randy's miracle with me. My mother underlined and circled the following passages on that page.

"After that He appeared in another form unto two of them." Mark 16:12.

" . . . but if you have had a vision of Jesus as He is, experiences can come and go, you will endure as seeing Him Who is invisible."

"Jesus must appear to your children as well as to you, no one can see Jesus with your eyes." (Note how my mother intentionally crossed out the word "friend" and inserted instead "children").

"O could I tell ye surely would believe it!

O could I only say what I have seen!

How should I tell or how can ye receive it?

How, till He bringeth you where I have been?"[7]

Appearing at the foot of my brother's hospital bed, Jesus answered in person that heartbreaking question Randy had asked as a young teen: "Am I one of God's forgotten thoughts?" Jesus called my brother, Randy by name. By name! Isn't that amazing! God knows each of us by name. "Yet thou hast said, 'I know thee by name'" (Exodus 33:17). No one is a forgotten thought of God! "Yet will I not forget thee. I have graven thee upon the palm of my hands" (Isaiah 49:15 16). God loves us beyond comprehension, and He knows our names, and He knows the plans that He has for us. Jesus answered Randy's question, and Jesus answered my mother's prayers. Praise God!

"I trust you and your brothers to decide what to put on my tombstone. All that matters to me is that I'm buried next to your father." My mother said this to me during one of my final visits to Florida. Even though it was evident that she wouldn't live much longer, I was still in denial and refused to even think about an epitaph. Shortly after my mother's death, we needed to make a final decision about her tombstone. After a silent prayer, I knew exactly in my heart what the lasting words should be — words from the Word of God, words that would reflect the simplicity of her faith, words that would teach, and words that would state the legacy of her life.

These are the words engraved on my mother's tombstone: *"Pray without ceasing"* I Thessalonians 5:17 .

Comfort

"*The grace of the Lord Jesus Christ be with you all.*" 2 Thessalonians 3:18

"*Now our Lord Jesus Christ himself, and God, even our Father, which hath loved us, and hath given us everlasting consolation and good hope through grace, Comfort your hearts and stablish you in every good word and work.*" 2 Thessalonians 2:16, 17

"*For this cause we also, since the day we heard it, do not cease to pray for you, and to desire that ye might be filled with the knowledge of his will in all wisdom and spiritual understanding; That ye might walk worthy of the Lord unto all pleasing, being fruitful in every good work, and increasing in the knowledge of God; Strengthened with all might, according to his glorious power, unto all patience and long suffering with joyfulness.*" Colossians 1:9 11

"*Now the Lord of peace himself give you peace always by all means. The Lord be with you all.*" 2 Thessalonians 3:16

Counsel

• Face it! . . . We live in a *fallen world* and because we do . . . *Grief* becomes an unwelcome companion with the human experience. Grief's footprints are found on every page of human history. For God's people, the remedy for grief is found in God's Word. Interesting that the first time we find the subject of grief in the Scripture is in Genesis 6:6: "And it repented (sorrowed) the Lord that He had made man on the earth, and it grieved Him at His heart." This verse is interesting because it speaks of God, rather than man being in grief. So the first occasion of the mentioning of grief in Scripture is Godward, not manward. I do not buy into the false teaching that the God of Scripture is emotionless as in stoic (unaffected by joy, grief, pleasure, or pain). Why would the [Christian] believer be commanded: "And grieve not the Holy

Spirit" (Ephesians 4:30), if He could not be grieved? Because our wonderful Lord was "acquainted with grief" (Isaiah 53:3) He certainly is with our grief. I would direct the believer to the two *major* sources for God's remedy for man's grief: first, is the infallible-inerrant Word of God. Here you will find a God who sees all, knows all, and understands all concerning your grief. Be assured . . . He will supply you with His glorious *grieving grace*. The second source is the *bridge of prayer*. This bridge will lead the believer from man's *nothingness* to God's *everything* . . . from man's *emptiness* to God's *fullness*. In conclusion . . . may I say, a believer may have the Word of God in his *hand* and even in his *head* . . . however it is when he has it in his *heart* that it becomes effective in his life (Psalm 119:11.)

Dr. F. William Chapman/Evangelist Bill Chapman Evangelistic Association

(On a side note, Dr. Chapman was one of my mother's students in a high school English class she taught in Florida.)

CHRONICLING

What legacy did my loved one leave?

What can I do to honor his/her legacy?

What do I want to leave as my legacy?

How has prayer touched my life?

Are there people in my life that I could be praying for? If so, please pray for them:

Dear Heavenly Father,

Chapter 11

Leaving a Legacy

Faith is the "white cane" for blind existence.
Beyond this single instant of life I am totally
    blind.
The maze ahead is obscured in darkness; each
    step holds potential terror.
But Faith goes before me to feel out the way that I
Might with confidence continue my journey.
Faith cannot see, but it can feel and conveys the
Message of having sensed the security of a safe
    surface upon which to tread.
Thus, with faith in my hand I need neither
    grope nor
Fear the terrors of darkness; for faith leads step
By step along the path to God.[1]
— CAROLYN RHEA

"God's trains run on time."

This was my dad's life quote — a reflection of unwavering faith in God's plans and in God's perfect timing. Those were always his words of encouragement for my discouragement. My dad lived his faith as an action verb — not simply a noun. He would often say, "I faith you, God."

My dad left many footprints of faith for me to follow throughout my life, and I would like to share four of those with you, dear reader: Faith, Hope, Love and Forgiveness. These have all become my landmarks in my life, and I hope that my father's footsteps of faith will provide comfort and direction for your journey too.

FAITH

Less than two weeks before my father died in Paris, I had flown from New York to West Palm Beach for Labor Day 1990 to plan my February wedding in Florida. My dad spearheaded the efforts to finalize venues and menus for the rehearsal dinner and reception, determine the most economical lodging options for guests, and select floral arrangements. He even pored over the menu options at The Governors' Club where the wedding reception took place and decisively chose those items that would make the most delicious presentation. He was a gourmand decades before it was trendy to be a foodie. My dad was pleased that Dave had asked him to select the place and menu for the rehearsal dinner. Daddy immediately thought about The Brazilian Court — a lovely historic landmark hotel in Palm Beach that turned out to be the perfect place for such a special evening. He chose poussin as the featured dish. Although one of my college majors was in French, I had not studied the culinary terms, but I assumed it was a fancy preparation for chicken. While walking back to the car, I asked my dad exactly what poussin was. "It's a baby hen," he answered, "and the chef's preparation will make it a succulent dish that your guests will enjoy." My stomach twisted momentarily when I heard the words *baby hen*. I must confess that even though I now host Kitchen Chat, the Internet radio show, I did not inherit my father's adventurous gene for cuisine. But of course he was right. Months later, the guests thoroughly enjoyed the poussin that my dad had selected for the menu.

An even bigger decision awaited us during that quick weekend of planning my wedding. Although he and my mother were members of First Baptist Church, my dad thought that a smaller and more intimate setting for my wedding would be more in line with my plans. He called Jeane O'Brien, a dear family friend who at the time worked for the rector at The Episcopal Church of Bethesda-by-the-Sea. She encouraged us to visit the church and would take us on a personal tour. My dad was right. This breathtaking Gothic church was the perfect setting for my wedding. Royal palm trees lined the front entrance of the church, and a splendid courtyard led to a private garden in the back.

September sunlight streamed through the stained-glass windows and imbued a sacred stillness within the sanctuary.

"May I have the honor of escorting you down the aisle?" my dad asked with a sparkle in his eyes, "This can be our practice run." We linked arms. With shoulders back and gallant steps, my dad walked me down the aisle of the church right to the altar where I was to be married. My mother and Jeane watched from a pew. With a twinkle in his bright blue eyes and perhaps a hint of a welled tear, my dad said, "And this is where I give you away with my blessings." He then kissed me on the cheek. Less than two weeks later he died in Paris. On my wedding day, my oldest brother, Claude, was the one who officially walked me down the aisle for the ceremony. However, in my heart, I knew that my dad had already given me away at the altar with his blessing.

My final conversation with my dad took place at a local McDonald's during my quick Labor Day weekend visit to Florida. My dad and I picked up Chee Chee at the assisted living home where she resided so we could stop for a quick cup of coffee before they dropped me off at the airport. My mother insisted that I spend some special time with them on my own. Chee Chee had always enjoyed the afternoon tradition of coffee with friends or family. Since her eyesight had waned at age 94, she asked my dad to read a letter she had just received in the mail. My dad obliged and read aloud the letter from her friend in Missouri.

The letter shared the sad news about the passing of one of Chee Chee's close friends. Wiping tears from her eyes, she excused herself and headed to the restroom. My dad folded the letter and slipped it back into the envelope. "Your grandmother has often mentioned that she is afraid of dying," he said peering across the top of his reading glasses. "I just want you to know that I am not afraid to die. I have faced death several times," Daddy paused for a moment, "and I even had a near-death experience." I took a sip of coffee as an act of avoidance and silently wondered if that event had occurred during his colon cancer surgery, his heart attack, or during his pituitary tumor surgery.

I often wish I had summoned the courage in that moment to ask my dad about his near-death experience, but I didn't want to hear him talk about his almost having died. He was always so vibrant and joyful in life and, as an adult child, I wasn't ready to hear anything that involved my dad coming close to death. I could not fathom the possibility of losing him. However, my curiosity could not be fully restrained as I remember thinking, *Oh, I'll ask him about that some other time. Maybe even during Christmas break.* Dave and I planned to spend Christmas with my parents in Florida and register for our wedding license. Hearing about my dad's close brush with death would have been easier to bear with Dave sitting next to me. Sadly, I never had the chance to ask my dad about his near-death experience. I silently let that incredible opportunity slip away and that is one of my greatest regrets.

My dad, however, continued this unusually poignant conversation at McDonald's even when I remained silent on the subject. As I wrapped my hands around the coffee cup, my dad looked at me with an inexplicable brilliance in his blue eyes. With intentional directness and inspirational calmness in his voice, my dad stated once again, "I just want you to know that I am not afraid to die." Those words lingered in the air like a four-count rest in a musical score. "I have lived a full life," he continued, "and as a Christian I know that death is just the beginning. Because of my personal faith in Jesus Christ as our Lord and Savior, I have the blessed assurance and gift of eternal life. And so do you." Chee Chee came back to the table at that moment and we soon headed to the airport.

During intense moments of grief, I often return to that final conversation with my dad and replay his words in my mind. I sometimes wonder if perhaps he had an inclination that his time was drawing near — thus the rush to help me fully plan my wedding, walk me down the aisle, and share his testimony and accepting peace about death. Whatever the case may be, I am grateful that God granted those special moments with my dad — moments that provided a firm stepping stone for my own personal faith journey.

HOPE

My dad's hope in Christ was the foundation for his unwavering faith. He always quoted, "Only he who sees the invisible can do the impossible." And one of his favorite Bible verses — the one which is inscribed upon his headstone is: *See, I am doing a new thing! Now it springs up; do you not perceive it? I am making a way in the desert and streams in the wasteland"* (Isaiah 43:19).

He truly had a God-given vision to recognize the possible in what seemed impossible. He would then encourage others to fearlessly step with faith to pursue God's purposeful plans. Much of today's campus of Palm Beach Atlantic University reflects my father's vision for this special college. Instead of building what was then the typical concrete campus, my dad envisioned beautiful stucco buildings with Mizner tiled roofs that would complement the environs of the Palm Beaches. He worked with an excellent architectural design team and together they designed a master plan for the campus.

I strongly believe that my father's gift of encouraging others to step with faith is what ultimately brought Chee Chee peace about her own impending death. She always told me she wanted to live to be at least 100 years old so Willard Scott would show her picture on "The Today Show" and wish her a happy birthday on-air. She almost made that milestone. Chee Chee passed away in April 1992 at age 96. She had expressed many times to my parents that she was afraid to die. After my dad's death, Chee Chee remained in the assisted living home, and my mother continued to care for her, taking her to doctors' appointments and spending time with her. They were a comfort to each other. While Chee Chee was in the hospital for congestive heart failure, I called her from New York. At that time, I didn't realize that Chee Chee was about to die. Providentially, I had already planned to visit my mother and grandmother that same week en route to meet Dave in Tampa where he was on a business trip. Dave and I had then planned to have a short vacation on the Gulf Coast. "I will see you in just a few days, Chee Chee," I emphasized on the phone. "Please hurry, honey," she urged, "I will wait for you."

The next day she slipped into a coma-like state and was moved to a nursing home/hospital. There was nothing else that could medically be done. When I arrived in Florida, my mother met me at the airport and tried to prepare me for Chee Chee's deteriorated health. I dropped off my suitcase and then borrowed the car to visit her. On the way to the nursing home, I picked up a cheerful flower arrangement. No matter what my mother had said, I still wasn't prepared to see Chee Chee in this condition. I had never sat in silence with my grandmother. Chee Chee always had the gift of gab. Her professional career as one of the earlier telephone operators for AT&T was a perfect fit for her. She loved to talk, and I loved to listen to her stories, latest happenings, and anecdotes. She was always chirping the latest news from Missouri or chatting about the new television shows.

Like my dad, Chee Chee always exuded a youthful vibrancy. No one ever believed her real age — including a policeman! I shall never forget driving her to pick up some blouses at the drycleaners. She was 89 at the time, so I pulled curbside in front of the storefront and waited for her there. Of course a policeman stopped behind me with flashing lights and said, "You can't park here. I'm going to have to ticket you." I stepped out of the car and explained that I was waiting for my elderly grandmother who was picking up her dry cleaning. "She's 89," I expressed with a tone of concern. At that moment, Chee Chee sauntered toward the car. She always looked stylish with trendy clothes and hair and makeup done.

The policeman raised his eyebrow, "Is this your grandmother?"

I of course said, "Yes."

The policeman then remarked, "There's no way that your grandmother is 89 years old." With feigned shock and a quick chuckle, Chee Chee said, "Of course I'm not that old."

As Chee Chee got in the car, the policeman gave me a parking ticket! She of course felt guilty about the little lie and offered to pay for my parking ticket. That was the Chee Chee I had always known.

Her silence in the nursing home was deafening. Yet, somehow she still exhibited her independent spirit by tugging the oxygen tube from her nose. She couldn't speak or open her eyes, but I know in my heart she sensed my presence. I rubbed her feet and called for the nurse to moisten her lips and swab the roof of her mouth. For the first time ever, we had a one-sided conversation as I talked and visited with her for a long while. I told her how much I love her. Her breathing was shallow yet labored. Just like she promised on the phone, Chee Chee waited for me.

That evening my mother gave me Chee Chee's opal ring. "But she loves this ring," I argued, still in denial that Chee Chee would soon die. "I know she wants you to have it," Mother replied with her signature graciousness. "And, Meg, there's something I need to tell you." Her face radiated an eagerness that I had not seen in awhile — at least not since my father died. Nodding my head, I encouraged her to continue. "The other day at the hospital Chee Chee kept calling out your father's name over and over. Claude! Claude! She was yelling so frantically that I had to close her hospital room door," my mother explained. "She seemed almost frightened. Then suddenly, she quieted down and started singing at the top of her voice 'When we all get to heaven what a day of rejoicing that will be. When we all see Jesus . . .'" My mother's eyes brimmed with tears. "This was the first time I had ever heard her sing. It was almost as if your father was ministering to her with music by singing that specific song with her." Mother then described how Chee Chee relaxed after singing aloud and then quietly slipped into a coma. I blinked back tears at the thought of my father helping Chee Chee overcome her fear of death by singing about the happiness of heaven. My mother's story comforted me after Chee Chee passed away a little more than 24 hours later.

I treasure my mother's poem "Heaven."

HEAVEN

I know that you're in heaven, dear.
How wonderful it must be!
A place where God's pure love
Surrounds each one,
Where Earth's tears are wiped away,
And joy and praise are everywhere!
Surely there is music there,
And you are singing in the heavenly choirs!
You're with Christ, our Savior,
Who led you safely there,
And you're experiencing the Heavenly Father's love!
Earth- time has ceased to be —
There in eternity!

Have you seen our families, dear?
Are you with your parents now?
Have you seen my mother and father?
And have you met my sister Margaret?
What about your friends who've gone before?
Can you see me now, my dear?
Are you missing me as much as I am missing you?
Or has heaven filled that void?
Are you burdened for me in my grief?
Please don't grieve for me.

I relinquish you to enjoy heaven.
And your great rewards
And to serve God in His new ways
Of ministry and worship.
When your mother was near death,
She kept calling you by name.
And then I heard her sing,
"When we all get to heaven,
What a day of rejoicing that will be..
When we all see Jesus . . . ."
(I'd never heard her sing before!)
Was that your answer
To her plea for help with dying?
How like you to speak through music!
Please sing to me!
My earth-years will pass
And our spirits reunite,
For love is eternal and does not die.
I'll see you in heaven, dear![2]

"Heaven" is one of my favorite poems from my mother's books.
What a blessing to have in writing this amazing experience of Chee

Chee singing "When we all get to heaven . . ." My heart can only imagine my parents' reunion in heaven. I like to envision that my dad greeted my mother with a song, a smile, and a sweet kiss. Then linking arms, with shoulders back and gallant steps, my dad walked her through the gates of heaven to safely lead her home. Hope in Christ was the foundation of his faith.

LOVE

Stacked inside a moving box, I found my parents' love letters. Hundreds of them. I of course have not been able to read every single one, but I have read enough to recognize what I always knew. They shared true love.

My parents met in Hawaii where they both served as student missionaries during the summer of 1949. My mother represented the Florida Baptist Student Union (BSU), and my dad represented Missouri BSU. This was a trip that almost didn't happen for my mother. Her parents trembled at the thought of their now only child flying across the Pacific to be a summer missionary only one year after they had lost their Margaret. In fact, her parents refused to sign the permission form that my mother needed for this mission trip. Yet stepping with faith, a dear friend signed the permission form on my mother's behalf. A long distance courtship continued after they returned to the mainland and back to college — my mother was at FSU, and my dad was at William Jewel in Missouri.

In her final book, my mother highlights some of the most meaningful excerpts from four decades of her love letters from my dad.

LOVE LETTERS

Darling, what treasures I'm finding in some of the
Boxes I'm going through: letters I wrote you and
Letters and notes you wrote me! Often, when you
Were going away, you'd leave a note on my pillow.

Several of your letters opened with these lines from our favorite love poem:

> "I love you not only for what you are but for what I
> Am when I am with you."*

After the bus in which you were riding back to College was in an accident, you wrote:

> "It's strange how, as I thought the end of my life was
> Near, I sent my thoughts of love winging to you. I love
> You not only in this life but in that one to come."

During a crisis time in my life, you penned these Words to me:

> "Three certainties, my love — even during the flood
> Times of life: One, God is able. Two, God knows your name and cares. Three, God loves you and so do I! Be at peace then. Rest upon His timing. This too Shall pass."

You shared these thoughts when we were seeking God's will for your life-ministry:

> "You know, sweetheart, I've been thinking a lot lately about what real success is. I used to believe it would be in some important post — but my concept of success has changed. True success is serving God to the best of your capacity in the place where He wants you to be."

And from Santiago, Chile, you sent me the gift of this treasured message:

> "Darling, the drive to serve God has sometimes caused me to seem unthoughtful. For this I ask your forgiveness and understanding. You have given me the opportunity and freedom to put Christ as pre-eminent. In so doing, our love has more dimension. Please accept by heart and my love — even across these long miles that separate us today."

In one of your notes you greeted me this way:

> "Good morning, love. It's a beautiful day! May you know bottom-line that God is on His throne and all is right. Hang in there today, and always know that I love you eternally!"

Thank you, darling. Though you are gone, you still speak to my heart.[3]

*Roy Croft, "Love," *The Best Loved Poems of the American People*, Hazel Felleman, ed. (Garden City, NY: Doubleday, 1936), 25.

How exciting to find the original letters that my mother highlights in her poem. The love note penned after my dad's bus accident had an additional enclosure that was actually written on the back of a Driver's Daily Log for Southwestern Greyhound Lines in 1951:

"In a ditch"
6 miles East of Marshall, MO

Hi, Sweet

Guess what — our bus has been in an accident — a car in front of us turned around and around on the slick highway and the bus tried to miss him and consequently we turned round and around, slid off the highway and barely missed going into a pond. Feel the Lord's hand was upon us — a few feet on the other side is a deep ravine and about 10 feet on our right is another deep ditch. We stopped just at the right place. No one in the car was injured, just mashed it up a bit. Threw some of us onto the floor base in the bus. Right now we're waiting for the wrecker to come. We're already an hour late — just hope I can make it to Columbia on time for the broadcast. Bye sweet — will mail this from Columbia.

Atop the left corner of the envelope that contained my dad's following love letter from Chile, my mother wrote: *Very important! My personal treasure.* This is the full context of that special letter:

October 12, 1967

My darling —

It's October 12 — the 9th anniversary of my bout with cancer. I woke up early this morning and during my quiet time have been thanking God for the second chance He afforded me. I can never put into words how much you've meant to me through the experience in the hospital, the weeks of recuperation and the years of adjustment that have followed. I don't dwell on the thought of it, of course, but I do realize how much it's demanded of you. I thank you Carolyn for being my wife, my helpmate, mother of our children, my love.

The drive to serve Him has sometimes caused me to seem unthoughtful. For this I ask your forgiveness and understanding. You have given me the opportunity and freedom to put Christ as pre-eminent. In so doing our love has more dimensions. Please accept my heart and my love — even across these long miles that separate us today.

Abidingly yours,

One of my dad's final notes to my mother was an anniversary card dated August 26, 1990, less than a month before he died. Beneath the date he wrote "(39 wonderful years later)."

My dad had a unique way of communicating his love for others while at the same time sharing words of wisdom. I keep two special letters in my Comfort Box. My dad wrote the following letter to me during his trip to Israel in late December 1982.

My dearest daughter Meg,

Somehow this morning I feel especially close to you — even though thousands of miles separate us. As I sit here on this snowy, cold morning in Israel, and as I reflect back upon the events of the past few days, the hustle and bustle of Christmastide 1982, the trip to Birmingham and the Poinsettia Ball with its beauty and significance, I somehow wanted to take a few moments and write on a heart-to-heart basis and communicate with you. As a father, I must tell you how lovely you were on Tuesday evening at the Ball. You literally radiated a loveliness and charm as you moved so easily from group to group and person to person. How proud I am to observe you in action and to realize my little gal has moved into beautiful young womanhood — and . . . that she has learned the important lesson of life — MAKING OTHERS FEEL IMPORTANT. Beyond the sheer loveliness of the "dress of the evening" (which I felt and am convinced was the prettiest one there) was the realness of you as a person. Your personhood is coming along nicely. As a father, I revel in your intellectual and spiritual maturation.

During the new year of 1983 I want to make a pledge to you. I am going to pray in a most special way for you each day. I am specifically going to claim from God for you: 1) ABOUNDING CREATIVITY; 2) INNOVATION in your studies and career discoveries; 3) SIZZLE ("It's not the steak that attracts the diner; it's the sizzle.") Sizzle is that "extra something" that turns ordinary into extraordinary!; 4) PROFESSIONALISM in your emerging role as a productive society member — and your upcoming senior year of college; 5) MANAGEMENT of your time, talents, creativity, innovation, sizzle, and professionalism. (Management will help you place new ideas, new outlooks, and new skills into a quality productivity); and of course, 6) I wish you LOVE — for yourself, your friends, and for the special one guy He is preparing for you.

Blest wishes my dear,
Your Dad

I am thankful that my dad had the opportunity to meet the man he had prayed for me to meet: My husband, David McSweeney. My dad's final written words of wisdom for me were on the engagement card that I received after my visit in Florida. This is what my dad wrote inside the card:

My dear Margaret and Dave

How happy we are for you both. As the days grow closer we feel the excitement growing. Life is really complete as you join your two lives into one. My word to you both is this . . . after almost 40 years, love grows greater and fuller.

Abidingly — Dad

Dave and I have been married for more than 20 years, and my dad's words are indeed true — that love grows greater and fuller. And Dave's love has helped me through some of the most difficult days of my grief. Love is an essential footprint of faith.

FORGIVENESS

Before catching a taxi to the Charles de Gaulle Airport in Paris, my dad and his business colleague stopped at Notre Dame Cathedral. With reverence, my father lit a candle and prayed for the person who had wronged him during a business deal. His final lesson to me was that of forgiveness — just hours prior to his death.

One day I hope to visit Paris and light a candle at Notre Dame Cathedral in memory of my father. Meanwhile, as friends travel there, I always ask them to light a candle in memory of my dad. Several years ago, Sandy, a dear friend and former neighbor, moved to London with her husband and two daughters. When she told me they had plans to visit Paris, I asked if she could please light a candle at Notre Dame Cathedral in memory of my dad. During her quick trip back to Illinois, Sandy and I met at the local McDonald's with our daughters who are the same ages and are close friends. She had brought a Christmas gift for me. Unwrapping the box, I gasped when I saw what was inside. It was an actual candle from Notre Dame Cathedral! Sandy told me that she kept her promise and had lit a candle. Then, she went into the gift store to purchase one for me. However, she noticed that the candles for sale were not the same as the one she had lit in memory of my dad. Sandy then spoke with one of the nuns and shared the story about my dad lighting a candle as an act of forgiveness. Sandy then asked if it would be at all possible to purchase one of the other candles. The nun insisted on giving Sandy an authentic candle to give to me as a Christmas gift. What a blessing this special candle has become in my life. Each year, I briefly light the candle in memory of loved ones and friends who have passed on, and I say a special prayer.

In December 2010, I lit the candle in memory of my brother, Randy. And in March 2011, I lit the candle in memory of Sandy. Yes, this special friend who had convinced the nun to give her a candle to bring back to Illinois lost her valiant battle against cancer. I miss Sandy. She was such a blessing in my life and in the lives of many people, including her precious daughters and her beloved husband.

My father's life lessons that he shared with me through his actions and his words continue to burn brightly in my heart like the special candle from Notre Dame Cathedral.

Forgiveness

Forgiveness is the fire in which I burn my neighbor's transgressions.
Because our lives are so close, I cannot help seeing
and feeling wrongs seemingly directed against me.
In the ensuing combat, however, love proves to be
Stronger than injured pride, and I toss the hurt
into the flames to be burned.
Only then can I bring my own transgressions to God
And ask that He too burn them in the blaze of
His great love.[4]
— Carolyn Rhea

Comfort

"For we walk by faith, not by sight." 2 Corinthians 5:7

"For therein is the righteousness of God revealed from faith to faith: as it is written, The just shall live by faith." Romans 1:17

"Blessed are they that have not seen, and yet have believed." John 20:29

"Now the God of hope fill you with all joy and peace in believing, that ye may abound in hope." Romans 15:13

"Beloved, let us love one another: for love is of God." 1 John 4:7

"By love serve one another." Galatians 5:13

"And thou shalt be secure, because there is hope." Job 11:18

COUNSEL

• I have heard it said well that "grief is the price we pay for having intimate relationships." All of us who are close to others, at one point or another, experience the pain of grief. Whether the death of a loved one, the end of a marriage, the crumbling of a friendship or the loss of a job . . . few, if any, are free to step around the valley of the shadow of death. Those who seek comfort from God are promised that they will never be abandoned . . . " Yea though I walk through the valley of the shadow of death, Thou art with me" is the powerful reminder from David's Psalm 23. That affirmation alone reminds us of two things. First, though we have that journey to face — it is not an end, but a journey "through," to the other side that holds for us hope, life, and resurrection. Second, when we make that journey — we are not alone . . . for "Thou" are with me. Grief can be a terrifying, lonely, empty experience, but holding the hand of the One Who Himself has tasted the sting of death on the Cross and made it to the other side of life beyond an empty tomb — holding that hand will surely help us to the other side.

The Reverend Russell J. Levenson, Jr., rector, St. Martin's Church, Houston

CHRONICLING

What footsteps of faith are important in my journey?

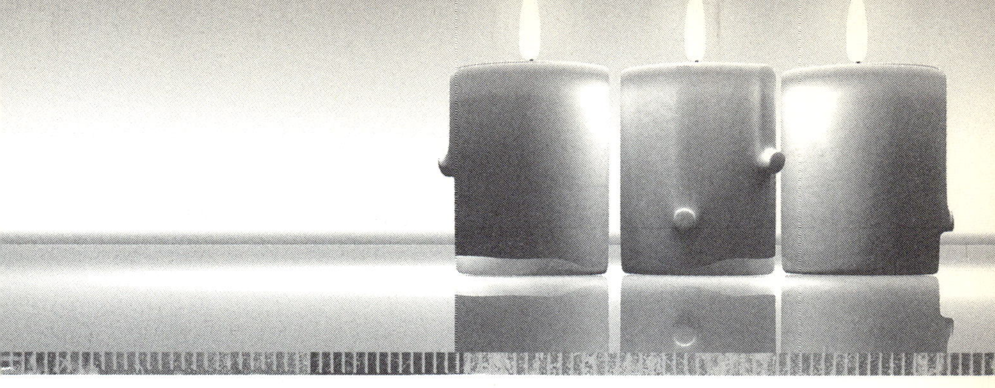

Chapter 12

Learning to Fly

I'm Earthbound —
Cumbered with duties
And overweight with love for earthly things.
Why should I feel such discontent?
Why should my soul want wings?
According to earth's laws
The bumbling bumble bee
Really shouldn't fly at all,
And yet it does.
So in the miracle of prayer
My spirit soars with God.[1]
— CAROLYN RHEA

"Just wanted to share with you my fresh inspiration and renewed determination to learn to fly in higher spheres and not to remain forever earthbound with grief."

The publisher's deadline was here; yet, I wasn't quite ready to press the "send" button. I confess that I still needed around 1,000 more words, but that wasn't what held me back. I felt in my heart that something was still missing. There was an important finale that still needed to be found and shared within these pages. I walked into my closet and scaled the clutter. I excavated my first treasure from a storage box hidden beneath tablecloths hanging in the back of my closet. (I don't know why I have tablecloths hanging in my closet—that's my next project!) Stuffed inside a long-forgotten and yet-to-be-filed manila folder within the box was a two-page, handwritten letter on stationery with an artistic rendering of two birds in a nest on the top right corner. The note was from my mother:

May 6, 1992

Dearest Meg and Dave,

I experienced one of God's parables this morning. Hearing a "thud" against the front screened door, I thought a golf ball had hit; and so I opened the door to survey the damage. There on the doormat lay a little yellow-throated bird, flat on its back after hitting the screened door while learning to fly! I saw the mother standing nearby, afraid to come near because the door was open and I was there. I closed the door, went inside and prayed for the little bird. When I opened the door again, it was gone — evidently recovered and trying once more to learn to fly.

I remembered our doves at the time of Claude's death and recalled how Randy had watched the young dove slam into the metal gate while trying to learn to fly.

And I remembered hearing Claude sing "His Eye is on the Sparrow."

I know God is near through Christ my Savior and will teach me how to fly alone without my beloved Claude. When I fall, He will help.

Just wanted to share with you my fresh inspiration and renewed determination to learn to fly in higher spheres and not to remain forever earthbound with grief.

I hope this reaches you for Mother's Day. I'm proud to be your mother, Meg, and your mother-in-law, Dave.

I love you dearly.

Mother/Carolyn

My mother's note is a treasured gift, and she did learn to fly in higher spheres so as not to remain forever earthbound with grief. Several years ago I, too, experienced one of God's parables that involved a bird. A robin's nest with a few tiny eggs was hidden beneath our deck. Our family watched with awe as the baby birds hatched and later learned how to fly. One Saturday afternoon, the final baby bird flew from the nest but landed on the trampoline in the backyard. This tiny creature flapped helplessly as it tried to escape through safety nets of the trampoline. Without hesitation, my husband climbed onto that trampoline and with a tennis racket gently scooped up that baby bird. Fearful at first, this bird didn't know that my husband was there to help, and it became frantic. Too exhausted to fight anymore, the bird at last allowed my husband to gently guide it from danger. With Dave's gentle strength, the baby bird at last flew high above the trees.

God's eye is on the sparrow, and His eye is always on us too. When our wings are too heavy and we crash into that sliding door of grief or we get trapped in the abyss of a trampoline and entangled in the safety net, God will provide the necessary strength so we can once again learn how to fly. Dear reader, I encourage you, and I will pray for you to find the courage and faith to surrender your grief and fears to the Lord. He waits for you with wings for your soul.

Before ending this book, I must share the second "hug from heaven." Within the clutter of my closet, I also found a copy of a letter my dad had written to a friend to comfort him on the passing of his father's death. As I read this correspondence, I could hear in my heart my father's gentle voice. In these moments of "recycled grace," may his words excerpted here comfort you as much as they have comforted me.

February 1, 1971

I am distressed to learn of your father's death. During these days following the initial shock and grief of separation, I am remembering and hurting with both you and your mother. I know that already the Comforter has come, even as Christ assured. As you both emerge from the icy waters of grief into the Spirit's warm and gentle "Gulf Stream of comfort," you can daily reflect upon the life your dad lived and the contributions he has made. On those rare occasions when our paths crossed, I was always a better person for having been with him. I sensed in him a gentleness, compassion and realness. Now you are heir to these fine qualities. Through your ever widening spheres of influence you can become a transmitter and disseminator of his finest attributes.

I sense with you that humanly speaking the now of separation is real and cold. When one's father slips away in death, a giant tree in our forest falls. A void is there that seems for a time to be unbearable. Yet — the Comforter will teach you all things . . . and bring all things to your remembrance . . . He will not leave you, nor forsake you. You are sustained . . ."

My heart pounded as I read this line: "When one's father slips away in death, a giant tree in our forest falls."

Yes, and when my father slipped away in death in Paris on September 19, 1990, a giant ficus tree on the college campus of Palm Beach Atlantic fell, too.

Thank you, dear reader, for the opportunity to share my journey with you. Each person's path through grief is different. I pray that you will feel encouraged and encompassed by the love, grace, and peace of our heavenly Father. "The LORD bless you and keep you; the LORD make his face shine on you and be gracious to you; the LORD turn his face toward you and give you peace" (Numbers 6:24–26, NIV). Embrace His grace!

With the ultimate theme of grace, I think it is fitting to close my book on grief with my mother's final pages that she wrote.

POSTLUDE:
GROWING IN GRACE

"But grow in grace, and in the knowledge of our Lord and Savior Jesus Christ. To him be glory both now and forever. Amen." — 2 Peter 3:18

At the time I wrote the following poem, "When Life is Felled," Claude liked it so much that he expressed a fervent desire for it to be read at his funeral someday. Our son, Claude Rhea III, read it at his father's memorial service. My husband's beloved ficus tree, felled by lightning on the day of his death, had become symbolic of his life and of his death.

The poem expresses my heart's desire to keep on growing through Christ my Redeemer, who strengthens me in all of life's circumstances and reminds me of the glorious welcome awaiting us at death!

WHEN LIFE IS FELLED

When Life is felled
In earth's forest,
May its rings reveal
Continuing growth.
And when death's final process
Transforms life's earthly trunk
Into heavenly scroll,
May Christ my Redeemer
See fit to write thereon:
Thou hast been faithful in the shadows.
Welcome to the Light![2]

Chapter 13

Grace in the Wilderness

Dear reader, I must insert a very poignant "Postscript" onto these final pages. After completing this book, I celebrated a milestone in life: I reached the half-century mark! As a 50th birthday present, my husband gave me the most wonderful gift imaginable — a trip to Paris so I could at last light a candle for my dad at Notre Dame Cathedral. How thankful I am that New Hope allowed me a few extra days before printing this book so I could share this unexpected blessing with you!

When my plane landed in Paris, my youngest daughter, Katie, and I walked into the Charles de Gaulle Airport. I blinked back the tears since this was where my dad had died nearly 22 years ago. At that moment, I made the decision not to go to the actual emergency room in the airport where he passed away. My purpose was to honor his *life* and *legacy*.

On March 27, 2012 — a mere five days after my 50th birthday, I made the long-awaited pilgrimage to Notre Dame Cathedral. The weather was spectacular. Sunny and close to 70 degrees. How fitting that the morning hours had been spent on a culinary tour of

Paris led by Wendy Lyn, founder of The Paris Kitchen and a fellow Samford University alumna. As I mentioned in a prior chapter, my dad was a "foodie" and he especially enjoyed French cuisine. I began my own culinary quest as I sampled cheeses, sausages, *fraises gariguette*, and fine chocolates. The fraises gariguette are French strawberries, which unofficially announce the arrival of spring. That morning, the first of these delicious and delicate strawberries just happened to be delivered from Provence to the outdoor market!

After the culinary celebration, it was time to head to Notre Dame for solemn contemplation. My friend May had traveled from London to join Katie and me for the food tour and for the candle lighting. Miraculously, the line was not very long to enter this historic place of worship. With reverence we walked through one of the majestic arched portals dating from the 1200s. My eyes took a few moments to adjust from the spring sunshine to the dimness of the interior grandeur. Placards placed throughout Notre Dame encouraged visitors to observe silence since people were praying. May, Katie, and I purchased several votive candles and lit each one to remember loved ones and friends who had passed. My friend May had recently become an adult orphan after losing her dad several months before.

As I lit each candle, held gently in my hands, I prayerfully reflected on the life and legacy of each loved one and friend who had passed away. As the candles burned brightly, I thanked God for my parents, Dave's parents, Chee Chee, and for my dear friend Sandy.

I also lit a votive candle on your behalf, dear reader, in memory of your loved one who has passed. As I lit your candle, I prayed for you. Although we may never meet, God knows your name, and He knows your needs right now. I prayed that you may feel His presence in your grief so you will know that you are not alone.

With the candles burning brightly on a circular stand, we proceeded down the long side-aisle that led to the altar. When I saw the large candles next to the altar, I audibly gasped. Tears streamed down my cheeks as my heart recognized that this must have been where my father had lit his candle and prayed. An oversized book lay open on a side-table in front of the candles. Small passages were written in a variety of languages. I assumed they were written prayers. Placing the wobbly pen in my hand, I signed my name and then poured words from the deepest place in my heart. Katie actually took a photograph of what I wrote in the prayerbook. I used almost a full page to record these thoughts:

Margaret McSweeney lit a candle in loving memory of her father, Dr. Claude H. Rhea Jr., who died in Paris on 9/19/90 while on a business trip. The last thing he did before heading to Charles de Gaulle Airport was to come to Notre Dame to light a candle and to pray for someone who had wronged him in a business deal. His final lesson to give during life was that of forgiveness. I am so thankful to the Lord for giving me such wonderful Christian parents. With this candle, which I now light, I remember and honor my beloved daddy and also my mother and brother Randy who now live eternally in heaven with our Lord and Savior, who forgave us of our sins. Praise God that we have eternal life and hope through Christ. Amen. 3/27/12.

I wept—publicly and profusely. Holding a long, white, tapered candle, I lit my father's candle on the altar. As my tears reflected the candle's flickering light, I looked up and saw the breathtaking beauty of filtered light streaming through a stained-glass Rose window from the thirteenth century. A glimpse of grace! At that moment, I sensed an indescribable peace. Just as God's brilliant light streams through pieces of broken glass, His eternal love also shines through our broken hearts with His gentle gift of grace.

"The people . . . found grace in the wilderness." JEREMIAH 31:2

Lord God,
Like Thy people, the Israelites,
Wandering in their wilderness long ago,
I, too, found Thy all-sufficient grace
In my wilderness.

Instantly torn asunder from my beloved,
My broken self plummeted into the dark
Wilderness of grief

But Thy grace —
Unmerited divine love and assistance —
Encircled me.
Underneath were Your everlasting arms.

Christ my Savior opened up the way
And taught me to walk by faith.
The Holy Spirit consoled me in my sorrow.

Tenderly, You brought me
Through the wilderness of grief,
Blessing me with grace gifts for my journey:
Love,   Strength,
Comfort,   Hope,
Forgiveness,   Healing,
Courage,   Peace.

Heavenly Father,
I love You. I worship You. I praise You!

I pray that other wilderness wanderers
Might find comfort in knowing
That in their wilderness
They, too, can find
Thy wondrous, all-sufficient grace!"
— CAROLYN RHEA

Endnotes

DEDICATION

[1]Carolyn Rhea, *Glimpses of God's Presence* (Nashville: Broadman Press, 1978), 16.

CHAPTER 1

[1]Carolyn Rhea, *My Heart Kneels Too* (New York: Grosset & Dunlap, 1965), 110. (Reverted rights to Carolyn Rhea.)

[2]Margaret McSweeney, "Visions of Faith." Used with permission.

CHAPTER 2

[1]Carolyn Rhea, *Such Is My Confidence* (New York: Grosset & Dunlap), 10. (Public domain.)

[2]Carolyn Rhea, *When Grief Is Your Constant Companion* (Birmingham, AL: New Hope Publishers, 2003), 1–3.

[3]Ibid., 22–23.

[4]Ibid., 42–43.

CHAPTER 3

[1]Carolyn Rhea, *When Grief Is Your Constant Companion* (Birmingham, AL: New Hope Publishers, 2003), 26–27.

[2]Claude Rhea, *With My Song I Will Praise Him* (Nashville: Broadman Press, 1977), 19–21.

[3]Ibid., 21–22.

[4]Ibid., 25.

CHAPTER 4

[1]Carolyn Rhea, *Such Is My Confidence* (New York: Grosset & Dunlap), 38.

[2]Carolyn Rhea, *When Grief Is Your Constant Companion* (Birmingham, AL: New Hope Publishers, 2003), 88–89.

[3]C. S. Lewis, *A Grief Observed* (San Francisco: Harper and Row, 1961; foreword by Madeleine L'Engle copyright © 1989 by Crosswicks, Ltd.), 10.

[4]Rhea, *When Grief Is Your Constant Companion*, 84–86.

[5]Claude Rhea, *With My Song I Will Praise Him* (Nashville: Broadman Press, 1977), 25–26.

CHAPTER 5

[1]Carolyn Rhea, *Healing in His Wings* (Nashville: Broadman Press, 1968), 58.

[2]Carolyn Rhea, *When Grief Is Your Constant Companion* (Birmingham, AL: New Hope Publishers, 2003), 68–70.

[3]Mrs. Charles. E. Cowman, *Streams in the Desert* (Cowman Publications, Inc., 1925, 1950), 268.

[4]Ibid., 61.

[5]Carolyn Rhea, *My Heart Kneels Too* (New York: Grosset & Dunlap, 1965), 110. (Reverted rights to Carolyn Rhea.)

[6]Margaret McSweeney, "In My Father's Arms." Used with permission.

[7]Rhea, *When Grief Is Your Constant Companion*, 132–34.

CHAPTER 6

[1] Carolyn Rhea, *Glimpses of God's Presence* (Nashville: Broadman Press, 1978), 40.

[2] Carolyn Rhea, *When Grief Is Your Constant Companion* (Birmingham, AL: New Hope Publishers, 2003), 80–81.

[3] Ibid., 30–31.

[4] Ibid., 72–73.

[5] Ibid., 9–10.

CHAPTER 7

[1] Carolyn Rhea, *Such Is My Confidence* (New York: Grosset & Dunlap), 80.

[2] Carolyn Rhea, *When Grief Is Your Constant Companion* (Birmingham, AL: New Hope Publishers, 2003), 128–29.

[3] Carolyn Rhea, *Healing in His Wings* (Nashville: Broadman Press, 1968), 60.

[4] Ibid., 12.

CHAPTER 8

[1] Carolyn Rhea, *Such Is My Confidence* (New York: Grosset & Dunlap), 12.

[2] Mrs. Charles. E. Cowman, *Streams in the Desert* (Cowman Publications, Inc., 1925, 1950), 237.

[3] Claude Rhea III, "Dark Chariots of Bright Grace." Used with permission.

[4] Cowman, *Streams in the Desert*, 164.

[5] Carolyn Rhea, *When Grief Is Your Constant Companion* (Birmingham, AL: New Hope Publishers, 2003), 188–90.

CHAPTER 9

[1]Carolyn Rhea, *When Grief Is Your Constant Companion* (Birmingham, AL: New Hope Publishers, 2003), 154–55.

[2]Mrs. Charles. E. Cowman, *Streams in the Desert* (Cowman Publications, Inc., 1925, 1950), 231.

CHAPER 10

[1]Carolyn Rhea, *My Heart Kneels Too* (New York: Grosset & Dunlap, 1965), 86. (Reverted rights to Carolyn Rhea.)

[2]Carolyn Rhea, *When You Pray* (Nashville: Convention Press, 1965), 3–5.

[3]Rhea, *My Heart Kneels Too,* 46.

[4]Ibid., 48.

[5]Ibid., 50.

[6]Carolyn Rhea, *Come Pray with Me: The Power of Praying Together* (Grand Rapids, MI: Zondervan, 1978), 36–37.

[7]Oswald Chambers, *My Utmost for His Highest* (Westwood, NJ: Barbour and Company, Inc., 1963), 100.

CHAPTER 11

[1]Carolyn Rhea, *Such Is My Confidence* (New York: Grosset & Dunlap), 2.

[2]Carolyn Rhea, *When Grief Is Your Constant Companion* (Birmingham, AL: New Hope Publishers, 2003), 192–94.

[3]Ibid., 136–38.

[4]Rhea, *Such Is My Confidence,* 32.

Chapter 12

[1] Carolyn Rhea, *My Heart Kneels Too* (New York: Grosset & Dunlap, 1965), 32. (Reverted rights to Carolyn Rhea.)

[2] Carolyn Rhea, *Glimpses of God's Presence* (Nashville: Broadman Press, 1978), 228–29.

Chapter 13

[1] Carolyn Rhea, *When Grief Is Your Constant Companion* (Birmingham, AL: New Hope Publishers, 2003), pp 224-226.

Additional Christian Living Titles from New Hope

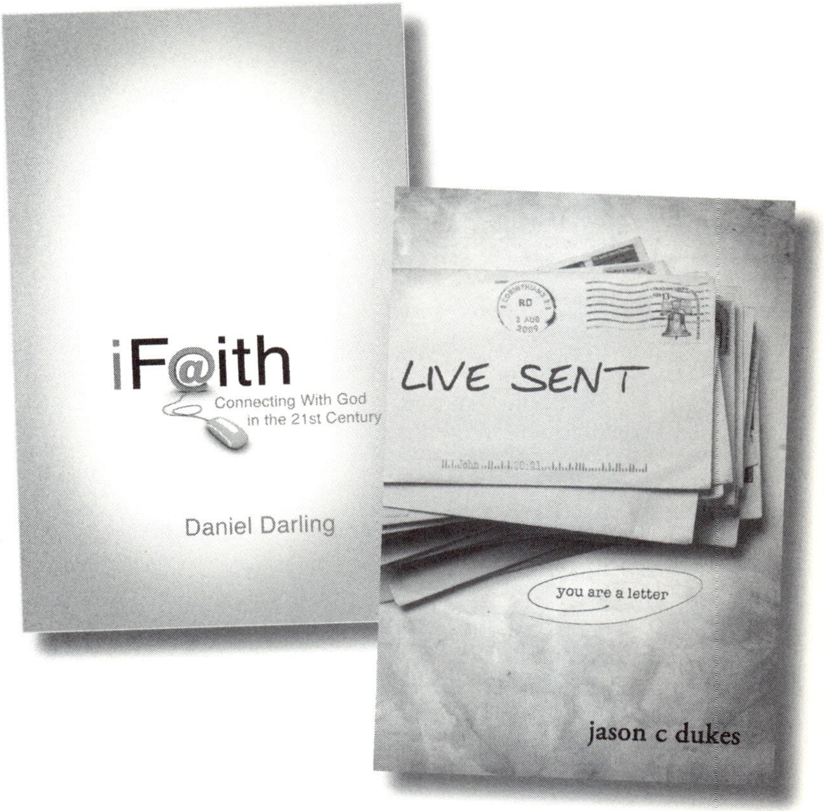

iFaith
*Connecting with God
in the 21st Century*
Daniel Darling
ISBN-13: 978-1-59669-294-7
N114131 • $12.99

Live Sent
You Are a Letter
Jason C. Dukes
ISBN-13: 978-1-59669-315-9
N114149 • $14.99

Available in bookstores everywhere.
For information about these books
or any New Hope product,
visit NewHopeDigital.com.

Use the QR reader on your
smartphone to visit us online at
NewHopeDigital.com

If you've been blessed by this book, we would like to hear your story.
The publisher and author welcome your comments and
suggestions at: newhopereader@wmu.org.